CROSSING BETWEEN TWO WORLDS
La via vecchia and *La via nuova*.
The Immigration Experience of
the Women of the Sgritta Family

FRANCES A. CALKA-NORTON

CASA LAGO PRESS
NEW FAIRFIELD, CT

Spuntini
Volume 4

This book series is dedicated to publishing those studies that are longer than the traditional journal-length essay and yet shorter than the traditional book-length manuscript. Intellectually, it is a light meal, a snack of sorts that holds you over for the full helping that comes with either lunch or dinner.

COVER PHOTO: Jennie's Family Portrait

ISBN 978-1-955995-08-5
Library of Congress Control Number: Available upon request

© 2024 Frances A. Calka-Norton
All rights reserved.
Printed in the United States of America

CASA LAGO PRESS
New Fairfield, CT

Table of Contents

Preface	vii
Introduction	1
Italy Before and After Unification	8
La via vecchia: Society and Class	20
La via vecchia: The Family	36
La via nuova	62
Conclusion	86
"I Dream of My Grandmother and Great Grandmother" by Maria Mazziotti Gillan	97
Bibliography	99
Appendix A	101
Appendix B	119
Index of Names	137
About the Author	139

In loving memory of my grandmother, Vincenza Giovanna Sgritta, and all of the Sgritta women whose stories live on in these pages.

Acknowledgements

"La famiglia non è una cosa importante. È tutto" (Family is not an important thing. It's everything. Italian Proverb. My lifelong dream has always been to write a book about my Italian family. As I think about this journey. it has been my family who supported me along the way. First, I'd like to thank my husband, Thomas Norton, and my beautiful daughter Katie Norton, for their patience as I have spent, and still spend, numerous hours researching our family genealogy. As a little girl, Kate spent numerous hours in the SHU library doing her homework as I did mine.

The story of the Sgritta women could not have been told without the love of my grandmother, Jennie Sgritta Cerulli and her sister Candida Sgritta Iacuzio. Their oral interviews formed the foundation upon which *Crossing Between Two Worlds* was written. The time I spent with them was priceless and know they are smiling down from heaven.

I also need to mention my cousin Richard Roberts who shares my interest in Sgritta genealogy and his great capacity to organize the information into a meaningful! format. We enjoy solving family mysteries together. I would like to thank Dr. Anthony Julian Tamburri, Dean of the John D. Calandra Italian American Institute of Queens College, CUNY, (my Cerulli cousin) and Stephen J. Cerulli, Doctoral candidate at Fordham University, (my Sgritta and Cerulli cousin) for believing the story needed to be told. A final thanks to

Casa Lago Press and Ella Carriero for their proofing of the text.

Between Two Worlds was originally written in 1997 as part of my graduate dissertation process at Sacred Heart University. I would like to thank Dr. John Roney, History Department Chair, my departmental supervisor for the project. Our lively discussions, as well as scholarly support and encouragement contributed to the success of this endeavor.

Preface

For as long as I can remember, I have been immersed in the customs, traditions, and culture of my mother's Italian family. My grandmother, Jennie Sgritta, held a special place in the family, as well as in my life. Almost twenty years ago, I began the task of researching the history of her family, the Sgrittas. This has not been easy because many of the older members of the family are now deceased. In addition, I have a limited knowledge of Italian and have had to rely on the many translations of others.

Vincenza Giovanna Sgritta, or just "Jennie," was born on September 18, 1904, the third child of Candida Lanzare and Salvatore Sgritta. In 1995 I completed writing her oral history to document her life's story. My grandmother was well past her 90th birthday at the time of these interviews. On some days she could remember things as if they had only happened yesterday. It was almost as if she would wake up and find her beloved husband, Giovanni (John), sleeping soundly beside her, or hear her five little children calling her name. These were the best days of Jennie's life, and it was with bittersweet memories that she recalled the stories of her past. These stories have played an integral role in developing this work.

On May 5, 1910, the first child of Salvatore Sgritta and his second wife, Antoinette Leone was born. Candida, or Candy as she is called, is a spry, little woman, who, at 87, continues to keep her own house, plant her own garden, and prune her grape arbor and fig tree. She has no qualms about getting on the bus and going across town to the store to buy wool for her crocheting. Among her daily routines was a trip to the rest home to see her Aunt Rosie who was 103 years old when she died in 1996. My great aunt's oral history has revealed that although she and Jennie were second generation Italian Americans, their attitudes and lives took on different directions.

As I interviewed more and more of the elderly Italian women in the Sgritta family, it became apparent to me that the reason the family had survived and prospered in the United States was that the women kept the family unit together by crossing between the two worlds of *la via vecchia* and *la via nuova*. They relied heavily on the behaviors, attitudes, beliefs, cultural traditions, and practices learned in the Old World in order to adapt to the modern industrial world of turn-of-the-century America.

Introduction

> ... Give me your tired, your poor,
> Your huddled masses yearning to breathe free,
> The wretched refuse of your teaming shore,
> Send these, the nameless, tempest-tost to me.
> I lift my lamp beside the golden door!
>
> —Emma Lazarus, "The New Colossus" (1883)

During the period of 1880 to 1921, millions of people throughout the world left their homes and emigrated to the United States. Although migration had always been part of human history, modern developments such as the railroad, the telegraph, and the steamship allowed individuals to travel faster, go farther and more cheaply than at any other time. In 1880 steerage passenger rates from Naples to New York were only $15; they grew to $28 in 1900 (Rolle, 3).

Prior to 1900, most immigrants came from northern and western Europe. The new wave of immigrants after 1900, however, came from southern and eastern Europe. They were strikingly different in appearance, language, religion, and culture from their predecessors.

The United States was in a period of rapid industrial growth which necessitated an ample supply of cheap, unskilled, and semi-skilled workers for mines and factories. The new immigrants arrived at a time when their labor resources were greatly needed and desired.

"La Merica" was where the street was paved with gold. Immigrant letters home to their families were filled with the wonders of America. Wages, for one thing, were two to five times higher than the Italians were paid at home. Agricultural workers in Italy were paid between 16 and 30 cents per day. Those who worked only during peak harvest season made between 50 to 60 cents per day. Miners were paid 30 to 56 cents per day. Carpenters received from 30 cents to $1.40 per day, or for a six-day week, from $1.80 to $8.40. In the United States, a carpenter could make $18.00 for a 40-hour week. The general laborer or *braccianti* would earn about $3.50 a week in Italy compared to $9.50 for a 56-hour work week in America (Iorizzo, 44).

Pamphlets and posters published by private companies, railroads and steamship lines further exploited this view of a land of riches, explicitly selling as many seats on railroads or ocean passages as possible (Kraut, 15). Italy had its share of those pursuing the travel trade. In the southern provinces, there were almost 160 agents with over 4,000 subagents who were often small village shopkeepers and tradesmen (Iorizzo, 16).

Although posters promising wealth and prosperity could be enticing, it is not enough, however, to lure someone from their home who is comfortable and content. There is no statistical evidence to indicate how influential this publicity was in the decision-making process of the Italian immigrants. The fact remains, however, that the United States offered economic opportunities that were unequaled anywhere else in the world, as well as the guarantee of personal freedom. There can be no doubt, therefore, that intolerable social and economic conditions critically affected the decision of individuals to leave their homeland (Kraut, 16). In his work, *The Huddled Masses*, Alan Kraut writes, "most often emigrants ventured abroad deliberately, not in spontaneous somnambulism occasioned by traumatic upheavals. They were not drawn from their homes, against their wills, as if by a distant magnet" (9). Kraut believes that emigration was one among various choices and not even the most popular in every region of southern and eastern Europe. He points out that "the vast majority of people in these places never left their communities" (9).

Historians have debated the question as to whether the immigrants were, in fact, the "downtrodden," "the uprooted," or "the huddled masses." The underlying theme in works such as Oscar Handlin's *The Uprooted* is that the "village was a harmonious social entity, in which the individual derived his identity and being from the community as a whole; the ethos of his village was one of solidarity, community and neighborliness" (Vecoli, 404). Immigration to Handlin was "a history of alienation and its consequences" (407). The immigrant in the New World became isolated and lonely because of "broken homes, interruptions of a familiar life, separation from known surroundings, the becoming of a foreigner and ceasing to belong" (Vecoli, 407). To Handlin, the immigrant no longer had the solidarity of his community and was cast upon his own resources as an individual (Vecoli, 405).

Rudolph Vecoli takes the opposite view of Handlin and critiques Handlin's thesis in his article, "Contadini in Chicago: A Critique of *The Uprooted*." Vecoli's position is that Handlin fails to recognize the unique cultural attributes of the various ethnic groups who emigrated to the United States. He states that "the idealized peasant village which Handlin depicts in *The Uprooted* did not exist in the southern Italy of the late nineteenth century" (404). Vecoli points out that the Italian peasant lived in a "rural city with a population of thousands or even tens of thousands" (404). These towns were not simple communities of peasants working the land but were rather complex communities with a social structure that included the gentry and middle classes as well. He states that while the Italian peasant may have enjoyed some solidarity with his community; the family truly provided the basis of peasant solidarity. "Each member of the family was expected to advance its welfare and to defend its honor, regardless of the consequences for outsiders" (405). It is this type of immigrant that most closely typifies the Sgritta family.

Between 1899 and 1910, 75 percent of all southern and eastern European immigrants were males, and 83 percent were between the ages of 14 and 44. Thomas Kessner states in *The Golden Door* that "the very low number of women and children pointed conclusively to a non-family migration and implied a primarily economic motive behind immigration" (30). Italian immigrants also fit into this pattern quite closely. For the years 1882 to 1883, for example, of the 64,000 Italian immigrants who entered the United States, 56,000 of them, or 88 percent were males. During the peak years of immigration, between 1880 and 1910, an average of 80 percent per year were males. Many of these immigrants were between 14 and 44 years old; less than 6 percent were over 44 years old, and less than 11 percent were under age 14. Kessner states that "the meaning of these figures is apparent. The Italian immigration was, by and large, a non-family movement of males in their productive years" (31) drawn primarily from the peasant towns of southern Italy. Kessner further states that "Italians emigrated largely for short-term economic motives. As the unusually high repatriation rates demonstrate, few intended to sever ties with their mother country permanently" (29).

Italian repatriation records indicate that over 80 percent of the returning Italians consisted of farm and common laborers. Ninety-six percent of those leaving the United States traveled third class. Of Italian-born professionals, only one in 250 returned to Italy. From these figures, it is apparent that those returning to Italy were not from the more prosperous classes.

The Sgritta family was atypical of these Italian migration patterns. It is significant that when Alphonse came to the United States in 1897, followed by Salvatore (my great-grandfather) in 1899, they chose to take their wives with them. If the father was the head of the Italian family, then the mother was the heart. We can be certain, therefore, that the Sgritta brothers intended to stay in America and make it their home.

My thesis is the Italian women played an integral role in the success of the Italian family in the United States by crossing between the worlds of *la via vecchia* and *la via nuova*. These women used the social attitudes, values, and customs of the Old World to create a firm foundation for the family in the New. These adaptations allowed Italian wives and mothers to continue to contribute to the social, economic, and emotional well-being of the family.

Carmen Fiore also suggests that women played significant roles in the family's immigration experience. In the foreword to the book *Voices of the Daughters*, he says:

> I believe that the Italian immigrant women have always carried the heavier load than the Italian male. They have had to be wife and mother, responsible for keeping the home clean, the clothes washed and ironed, the children presentable, the food prepared, but often they had to help support

the family as well. They did what was necessary. If they stayed home, it was sewing for a local clothing factory, or taking in laundry; if they had to, they left their homes to work in sweatshops, whatever it took to make money to help keep the family together — survival as a unit. (xix)

We must understand the world that the Italian woman came from to understand how she was able to adjust to her new life and role in the United States. Therefore, the first section of this study will be dedicated to "La via vecchia." Using Sgritta family oral histories and private papers, as well as the memoirs of other Italian women, we will look at what life was like for an Italian woman coming to the United States at the turn of the century. We shall compare and contrast the experiences of Jennie and Candida Sgritta and investigate why they had different experiences, even though they were both "second-generation" Italian Americans. We will also compare their experiences to women of other Italian families. In conclusion, we will look at ways in which Italian women, in general, and the women of the Sgritta family, in specific, adjusted their ideals and customs to those of the American community around them.

Italy Before and After Unification

The key to understanding one's present and predicting one's future, lies in knowing about one's past. This especially holds true when analyzing why certain customs, beliefs, and rituals were so crucial to the Italian men and women that they transplanted them to their new life when they immigrated to the United States in the last decades of the nineteenth century. By looking at the past we can see more clearly how Italian women could cross successfully between the world of the past and the world of the present by adapting traditional roles and social mores.

One of the first concepts that we need to understand is the idea that the Italian people, unlike the English or French, had no concept of nationality. The term "Italian" was a name given to the people who immigrated from the Italian peninsula by the Americans. These immigrants, however, did not see themselves as Italians but as members of a region or community. They were Calabrese or Neapolitans or Genovese. Until unification in 1861 Italy had been divided into small principalities or foreign controlled states which were more often concerned with shifting political alliances and their own rules and regulations. The government was seen, therefore, as a hostile and distant entity, interested only in excessive taxation and the recruitment of young men to fight in far-off wars. The absolute authority lies with the heads of the various families in the communities.

After the fall of the Roman Empire, a succession of invaders — the Lombards, Byzantine Greeks, Arabs, Normans, Catholic Germans, the French, and the Spanish — established permanent settlements in the Italian peninsula and gradually assimilated into the rest of the population. Italy became "the Western world's first great melting pot" (Mangione, 46). While the origins of the Sgritta family can be traced to Salerno, just south of Naples in the Campania region of Italy, to the year 1800, there is a good chance that they were among those who assimilated with these other cultures. The great assimilation of peoples and cultures in the area would significantly contribute to the differences between cultures and customs between Northern and Southern Italians. The need on the part of the native Italians to constantly adapt to intruders, however, resulted in the development of *l'ordine della famiglia*. Richard Gambino, in his book, *Blood of My Blood*, says that *"l'ordine della* famiglia was a system of social attitudes, values and customs that had proven to be impenetrable to the *sfruttamento* (exploitation) of any *straniero,* no matter how powerful their weapons or clever their devices" (27). *L'ordine della famiglia* would provide a valuable source of protocol for the Italian woman in her interaction with her new American neighbors.

Italy was quite different from her neighbors in Western Europe. While France, England and Spain were moving toward nationhood, Italy remained fragmented into numerous city-states, each with its own foreign policy and political agenda. Florence, Pisa, Milan, Venice, and Genoa were wealthy centers of commerce, the arts, and European life, especially during the Renaissance period. If the area was attractive to foreign powers in the past, it has became even more attractive now. These city-states often squabbled among themselves, taking sides against each other, and further weakening them. When several city-states asked for help from the outside, King Charles VIII of France was more than happy to help. In 1494, he marched his army into Italy. The city-states, in their weakened condition, could not hold back the French army. Although Charles eventually withdrew, it became all too apparent that Italy was ripe for the taking. For many years, France and the Holy Roman Empire would fight wars over the control of Italy.[1]

The French Revolution and the Reign of Napoleon Bonaparte had a profound influence on the Italian people. When the French king was overthrown

---

[1] In 1519 King Charles I of Spain, a member of the Hapsburg family, became Emperor Charles V of the Holy Roman Empire. In 1521 France and Spain went to war over rival claims to Italian lands. Spanish troops looted Rome and later took Sicily and Milan from France. By 1559, almost all of Italy was under Spanish influence and control. However, when Ferdinand I succeeded Charles, the title of emperor passed from the Spanish Hapsburgs to the Austrian Hapsburgs. By the early 1700's control of the area passed from the Spanish to the Austrians. Austria governed Milan directly and controlled the rest of Italy through local rulers loyal to the Austrian king.

and France became a republic, several secret societies formed in Italy that supported the establishment of an Italian republic. In 1796, Italy became the battle ground between the Hapsburgs and the French once again. Napoleon Bonaparte led his army into Northern Italy and drove out the Austrians. Wherever he went, Italian republics were formed with constitutions and legal reforms. When Bonaparte declared himself Emperor in 1804, part of Northern Italy became the Kingdom of Italy under his rule. The rest of Northern Italy was added to France. Although French rule lasted only 20 years, it was quite different from previous foreign control. Despite heavy taxation and frequent harshness on the part of the French, they also introduced representative assemblies and laws that were consistent throughout the country. For the first time since the Roman days, all Italians served in the same army and used the same currency.[2]

When Napoleon was defeated in 1814 by the major European powers, Italy became fragmented once again. The Congress of Vienna decided that in most cases Italy's former rulers would be returned to power. In the northwest, the royal House of Savoy returned to rule Piedmont and Sardinia as the Kingdom of Sardinia. In southern Italy, Naples and Sicily again came under the control of the Bourbons, a French

---

[2] See the following books for a history of Italy: Jerre Mangione and Ben Morreale, *La Storia: Five Centuries of the Italian American Experience,* Alexander DeConde, *Half Bitter, Half Sweet An Excusion into Italian American History,* Richard Gambino, *Blood of My Blood,* and Humbert S. Nelli, From *Immigrants to Ethics: The Italian Americans.*

royal family. The Papal States were returned to the Pope. Lombardy and Venetia were placed under direct Austrian rule and other states ruled by dukes loyal to Austria were established.

Although Austrian power was more firmly established in the Italian peninsula than before, progressive Italian lawyers, professors and liberal noblemen began to envision a united Italy free from foreign control. The "Risorgimento" movement was the nationalistic dream of four northern Italians — Giuseppe Mazzini, King Victor Emmanuel II of the House of Savoy, Count Camillo Benso di Cavour, the prime minister of Piedmont, and Giuseppe Garibaldi. The movement aimed to remove all foreign powers from the region and form a single, united Italian republic. It became apparent to the Italian patriots that the only way to get the reforms they wanted was to expel the Austrians from Italy.

In Piedmont Count Cavour began to initiate policies that would lead to a progressive, independent state. Sardinia became the spokesman for Italy against Austrian rule in various European councils. He established a defense agreement with Napoleon III in 1858. Austria, fearing that its control over Italy was weakening, declared war on Sardinia in 1859. Soldiers from France and Italy pushed the Austrians back as far as Venice. Any local rulers who had supported the Austrian king were expelled in local revolts. All of northern Italy, except Venetia, down to the Papal States were joined to the Kingdom of Sardinia. The push towards a unified Italy had begun.

In 1860, Giuseppe Garibaldi and thousands of volunteers sailed to Sicily to aid the Sicilians in their fight for freedom against the Kingdom of Naples. Garibaldi's small, enthusiastic army was called the "red shirts" and was successful in defeating the larger and more professional army of Naples. After a successful romp in Sicily, Garibaldi crossed to the Italian mainland and conquered southern Italy and the city of Naples. Several weeks later, he handed over the *Mezzogiorno* to King Victor Emmanuel, and the area was integrated into the Kingdom of Italy. Dominic Sgritta, who was born in 1841, was caught up in this time of political unrest. As a member of the bourgeoisie class, it is possible that he was among those who fought with Garibaldi.

Despite Garibaldi's efforts, the Italian peninsula would remain divided — socially, economically, and politically, for many years to come. The most serious problem confronting the new Italian government was that the regions of Northern and Southern Italy knew almost nothing about each other. The new Italian nation did not even have a unifying language. Only 2.5 percent of the population spoke Italian; the rest spoke the dialects of their various regions. In addition, feudalism took a long time to die in the *Mezzogiorno*. For almost 400 years the south had suffered the oppression of Spanish viceroys and Bourbon overlords. It was an agrarian economy and these foreigners found that it was best to keep their vassals in forced ignorance. It was to their advantage to keep communication between the various provinces and villages at a minimum. In essence, while "the well-to-do leaders believed they were making a revolution for the poor of the South, in reality they were making it for themselves" (Mangione, 57).

To the more industrialized, cultured Italians of the north, the area of the *Mezzogiorno* must have seemed provincial at best. Education in the South had been denied to the majority of the population, with schools being reserved only for the children of the wealthy. Travel in the Kingdom of the Two Sicilies had been restricted to within the kingdom only, and even then, a passport was required. There was an extreme lack of roads, which the Bourbons had blamed on their Spanish predecessors, but chose to do nothing about. Of a total of 1,848 villages, over 1,600 of them had no roads at all. Jerre Mangione, in his book *La Storia,* states that "in every possible way the southern masses were insulated from developments outside the boundaries of their circumscribed world that might inspire them to disturb the status quo" (46).

A deep hostility was provoked in the people of the south when, in 1861 the Turin government imposed the 1848 Piedmont constitution on all provinces in the kingdom, regardless of their particular needs. When the Southern Italians had voted in favor of annexation to the Northern Kingdom of Italy, they had expected that they would have some say in the government. It became apparent, however, that the government in Turin had no intention of sharing power with the South. Although there was an awareness that there was a pressing need to integrate the southern regions and provide for their participation in "national" life, every attempt was made to delay the process.[3]

Of all the edicts imposed by the Piedmont constitution, the one that created the most antagonism among the Southern Italians was the military conscription law which required seven years of military service for young men. To the peasants this was a severe loss of labor within their households.

In addition, peasants who had been considered too poor in Bourbon times to pay taxes, were now required to pay taxes for the first time. A tax was placed upon almost "every living animal the *contadino* has — his ox, his ass, and his pig" (Iorizzo 43). By the end of the nineteenth-century, Italy had the highest taxes in Europe.[4] Although they were the

---

[3] See Grazia Dore, "Some Social and Historical Aspects of Italian Emigration to America," *Journal of Social History*: "The rural areas were excluded in practice by confining the electorate to those who could demonstrate a knowledge of reading and writing and who possessed some, even if a modest income. This was at a time when the illiteracy rate was extremely high" (98).

[4] In 1868 a tax was enacted on the grinding of grains known as the *macinato*. The Southern Italians considered this grist tax to be discriminated against them because the higher taxes were paid on the grinding of wheat, which was the major grain in their diet. They believed that the Northern Italians, whose major grain was corn, was favored. Widespread opposition to the grain taxes led to the repeal of taxes on lesser grains in 1880 and at that time the tax on wheat was reduced. Although the *macinato* was done away with completely in

ones that were least able to afford it, the *contadini,* or peasants, and the *giornaliero,* or day laborers were faced with the highest taxes. Taxes were placed on buildings and land, and excise tariffs were placed on salt, sugar, tobacco, and liquor. In addition to taxes imposed by the central government, the people were subject to taxes levied on the local commune and provincial level; Humberto Nelli gives an insight into North-South relations in his book, *From Immigrants to Ethics: The Italian Americans*:

> Throughout history Southern Italy was exploited by invaders and conquerors but none victimized the region more than the government of the new Kingdom of Italy controlled by fellow Italians from the North. As far as the Southerner was concerned, the foreign domination continued, now in the form of a more efficient, oppressive, and ruthless government in Rome. (24)

Unification also adversely affected the industrialization of the South. By the turn of the century, Northern Italy made significant advances in wealth, trade and education. The South, however, remained stagnant. The government enacted tariff systems that benefited the North and virtually wiped out the southern industries that had developed in the decades before unification. Public works projects, such as

---

1884 and gave some relief to poverty, it did not greatly contribute to improving the lot of the Southern peasant.

the construction of roads and railroads, favored the northern and central regions of Italy. For example, the first extensive railroad to be built after unification went between Turin and Paris, instead of Naples. Mangione says, "While the rest of the nation was approaching the era of industrialization and, at the same time, improving the lot of its peasantry, the South was left to fend for itself" (Mangione, 75). He says further that the half measures adopted by the government to bring the *Mezzogiorno* into modern society did little to relieve the Southern Italians sense of betrayal that the new regime and the deputies who were supposed to represent them did little to fulfill the promises of Garibaldi. "The greatest deception was the regime's failure to provide them with the opportunity of acquiring enough land to put food on the table, so as to free them to some extent from the rapacious demands of landowners. If anything, the new regime, from the peasant's point of view, had created an even greedier landlord" (Mangione, 77).

Italy, once the breadbasket of the Roman Empire, was suffering from a slowdown, especially in the South, in the production of most foodstuffs, except for fresh fruit, tomatoes, fish and fresh vegetables. The soil in many places was difficult to work and not very fertile. Unlike Northern Italy with its flowing rivers and deep, natural lakes, Southern Italy almost completely lacked significant waterways. Rainfall, which occurred heavily in the winter and spring, combined with melting snow, running off the hills in torrents. The result was the depletion of precious topsoil and the development of malarial swamps in the lowlands. Drinking water was a rare commodity in many southern Italian villages. Often the only water source was the rain they might capture in rain barrels. During the dry season, some peasants fortunate to have wells with excess water, would strap barrels of it to their donkeys and sell it in bottles to their less fortunate neighbors. According to Mangione, irrigation development in Southern Italy would have improved its economy tremendously. The new government, however, chose to create these facilities mainly in the North. Of all artificially induced irrigation in Italy, only 8 percent was developed in the South (75).

Other factors contributed to the decline in the Italian economy. First, the influx of American and Russian grain into Italy greatly affected domestic wheat prices. Secondly, a subtropical fruit industry was developed in California and Florida, in the United States. Thousands of lemon and orange growers in Calabria, Basilicata, and Sicily were ruined. American imports of Italian lemons and oranges dropped off drastically because import tariffs were enacted to protect this new industry. Lastly, wine growers in the provinces of Apulia, Calabria, and Sicily suffered a similar fate when France enacted tariffs to protect her wine industry, thereby eliminating the primary source of Italian wine exports. An outbreak of the phylloxera plant parasite in the 1890s virtually destroyed most of the vineyards in Southern Italy and greatly curtailed the country's wine industry. As French wines began to replace the Italian product on the open market, thousands of farm workers were displaced.

Overpopulation put an additional strain on the already weakened economy and was a chronic problem in Italy. In 1881 it was 28 million, in 1901 it was 32 million, and by 1909 it was over 34 million (Nelli, 20). The population density in that year in the kingdom of Italy was 310 people per square mile. Only Belgium, the Netherlands and England had greater population densities; however, unlike Italy, they ranked as highly industrialized nations (19).

LA VIA VECCHIA: SOCIETY AND CLASS

Salvatore Sgritta was born into post-unification Italy on April 4, 1871, the first son of Dominic Sgritta and Angelina Sorrentino. Family history says that Dominic's grandfather worked as a civil engineer in the employ of the King of Naples. However, if one uses the dates mentioned in the brief history of Italy discussed above, it is quite probable that he participated in the governments set up during the brief reign of Napoleon. This Sgritta rose to prominence and earned his own coat of arms. The inscription beneath it has been translated into English as follows:

> Ancient *casata* deriving from Liguria and dispersed in various localities of the peninsula. Enjoyed a good social position and a main branch of the family was steeped in nobility. They have distinguished sons in various areas of human activity such as coming from civil magistrates, cultivating studies especially in law. (Sgritta Family Crest)

It is possible that this Sgritta met his wife in northern Italy, while on government business. She was tall, blond, and blue-eyed, traits which can still be seen in some of the Sgrittas today. This is very unusual because people usually looked to those of similar class in their communities as prospective marriage partners. It is also possible that this marriage began as one of convenience, used by this gentleman to further his career.

In the late nineteenth century, Italy's social system reflected the remnants of its feudal past. A closed, static society, there was virtually no way to move up the "social ladder," especially for the peasants. Historians Humberto Nelli and Leonard Covello agree that social aspects were, for the most part, determined by the existence of a strict caste system. Covello says that "not only was there a wide gap between the upper and lower brackets, but also within the subdivisions of the lower class itself, there was a rigid demarcation between various groups" (Covello, 78). Nelli states that "the population was divided between the few who were wealthy, socially prominent, and politically powerful, and the many, who were poverty-stricken and powerless. Also, unlike England, the middle class in Italy was virtually non-existent" (Nelli, 26).

There were strict distinctions within the peasant class between the *massaro*, the *contadini* and the *giornaliero*. Mangione believes that because the peasant had no way to break into the other classes of society, "the peasantry fell into the habit of turning against one another instead, thereby enacting a peasant caste system as rigid and heartless as the one imposed upon them by the gentry" (Mangione, 49).

The *giornaliero*, or day worker, was the pariah of peasant society, an outcast even among the peasants. Living in squalid huts on the outskirts of town, the *giornaliero* lived the life of a nomad, moving from place to place to find work. Great distances between the workplace and home allowed him to visit family occasionally. He, therefore, did not have a share in the local affairs of the town. Covello says of the *giornaliero* that "poverty, or rather his low status as taxpayer, usually excluded him from the right of suffrage, and lessened still more his already loose ties with the community" (Covello, 79).

The *giornaliero* was only a little better off economically than the town beggar. His primary interest in life, however, was to save what money he could so that he could rent a small parcel of land and break the line separating him from the next rung on the peasant social ladder. Covello further states that the *giornaliero* "was discriminated against not because of his occupation status, but because of a lack of money sufficient to enable him to buy a house of his own or to become possessor of even a small plot of ground, or to purchase a donkey, some animals and a few tools, possession of which would have made him eligible for a lease of land" (79). At the turn of the century, about 500 lire, or $100, would have been enough for the *giornaliero* to do this.

Although there was little to distinguish the *giornaliero* from the *contadino*, there was a strong solid social barrier between the two groups. The *giornaliero* was often referred to as a *cafone*, or low brow. Covello believes that this would indicate that "the social barriers between the two classes were rooted in divergencies other than differences in economic status" (80). One Italian American interviewed by Covello characterized the *giornaliero* as follows:

> The *giornaliero* was first of all a *cafone*, i.e. rough, ill-mannered. He showed no respect for the customs and traditions of the family and society. When he could get away with it he did not consider the rights or feelings of other people. He had no ideal to rise to. He was an unfeeling clod, too dull to think of finer things of life. He was engrossed merely in material pursuits. Nothing was sacred to him. A man of no soul. (80)

The *contadino* was economically better off than the *giornaliero* because through either ownership or lease they possessed a parcel of land and had a home in town or a *capanna*, or hut, in the field which often the family had inherited from previous generations. The *contadino* also owned various tools and animals. Giovanni Carano Donvito says in his work, *L'economia meridionale prima e dopo il Risorgimento*, that these items, although not intrinsically of great value, gave the *contadino* an advantage. "The possession of even primitive mobile property enabled the *contadino* to borrow money on its strength — while the laborer had no such advantage" (Carano Donvito, 83). The sudden acquisition of wealth or economic success of a *contadino* did not remove him from the class of peasant as long as he maintained his association with agriculture. A few members of the peasant class owned 40 to 50 acres of land. Their actual wealth was often greater than of the impoverished noblemen. Yet, as Covello says, "the wealthy farmer remained an inalienable part of the peasantry. He was still *contadino*" (Covello, 88). The difference in economic status was often recognized by the designation of the peasant as a *borghese* or *massaro*. Covello continues by saying, "As wealthy persons they enjoyed more dignity and were influential in the peasant life of the town. But in all other aspects their position was the same as that of the peasant group as a whole" (88).

There were no outward differences between the different peasants' groups. They all spoke the dialect of the region and wore the same traditional clothing. Although living conditions were generally the same, the *contadino* often cultivated a small patch of land as a garden and had, therefore, more variety in his diet. "The *giornaliero*, like the peasant, was addressed always by his first name, *(buon giorno,* Giovanni). More often, however, he was simply addressed by "*tu*" (an informal linguistic address). In some parts of the South, primarily in Sicily, the title of *Santu* (Saint) was added to his first name in sarcastic reference to the *giornaliero*'s absence of worldly riches" (Covello, 79).

Artisans, merchants, and small shopkeepers of the Italian towns made up the bourgeoise, or middle class. In southern Italy a middle class was almost non-existent because although feudalism had been absolved, many of the practices continued for a long period of time. There were either very large estates called *latifundi* that were owned by the gentry class, or extremely small plots owned by peasants, that usually could not even yield a livelihood for a single family. A medium sized estate virtually did not exist. The *artigiano* and merchant, who comprised as much as one-third of a town's population, can therefore be considered the middle class or bourgeoisie. Artisanal work was one of the most important sources of non-agricultural work.

Although, at times, shopkeepers and merchants were a little better off economically than the *artigiano* or artisan, they did not maintain any divisions between themselves. Intermarriage between these two groups was quite common. Artisans and merchants did not see themselves as rivals but came from the common traditions of the medieval guilds. The *artigiano* depended on the peasants and the upper class for his living. He was the mason, blacksmith, shoemaker, barber, tailor, or any other skilled craftsman who provided services requiring skill for the local community. The midwife was also considered to be part of the artisan class. Artisans commanded the respect of all the classes.

Each trade had master artisans who would teach the trade to others. The title *maestro* was only given based on an artisan's reputation as a skillful worker in his trade and on the basis of long experience. This privilege of *maestro* not only meant prestige within his group, but also economic gain. Meaningful work and commissions were not given to apprentices, even though they would be willing to work for lower wages. Covello states, "the training process of an artisan was not only education in the particular trade, it not only determined his future economic life but also set him up socially. Men with such training were *a priori*, or outstanding individuals in southern Italian society" (Covello, 93). The title *maestro* addressed any male member of the artisan's family, regardless of his work or economic status.

The son of an artisan would continue in the art or trade of his father. "He began as an apprentice at the age of ten, and often younger, becoming a shop boy *(garzone)*, then a worker *(lavorone)*, thus step-by-step establishing for himself a position of independence, the respect of his fellow workers, and the commendation of his elders in the community" (Covello, 93).

The difference in status between the *contadino* and the artisan was apparent in many ways. The peasant was in the majority of cases, illiterate, while many of the artisans could read and write and could do basic mathematical figuring. Although books and newspapers were relatively scarce in rural villages, religious texts, often about the lives of the Saints could be found in artisans' homes. Covello says "the artisan was a lover of music and was quite familiar with the fashionable tunes of his day and with the principle arias from the Italian operas. He never saw them, but through contact with the *galantuomo* class, from the local bands, or in his travels, he acquired knowledge of them and sang them with the aplomb of a connoisseur" (94). An artisan usually played a musical instrument, usually a mandolin or guitar.

The friends and relatives of the artisan were others like himself, small shopkeepers, and property owners. He attended Mass regularly and was a generous supporter of the Church. This increased the status of the artisan in the eyes of the clergy and, his conduct, to some extent reflected the moral norms of the community.

One of the main differences between the artisan and the *contadino* was the artisan's interest and participation in the political affairs of his town. Covello states that "the traditional adherence of the artisan to the ideas of political independence, as embodied in the ancient guilds and trade corporations, and his wider knowledge of affairs made the artisan, at the time of the Risorgimento, a liberal in a political sense. It is not surprising, therefore, that many artisans were active, both in the wars of liberation, and in the establishment of a politically united Italy after the Risorgimento." It also stands to reason that when things did not improve, it was the artisans who were among the first to emigrate to the United States.

Anyone who was not a fisherman, peasant, or artisan, did not do manual labor, and who at the same time enjoyed a prosperous life, was known as *galantuomo* (of Bourbon origin), *signorotto* (of North Italian origin), or as *cavallacci* (of Aragonese origin). The peasants also referred to the gentlemen class as *cappedi* (hats) because the men wore hats instead of the caps worn by the male members of the other classes. Covello describes them as follows:

> The priest, the doctor, lawyer, notary, druggist were also known as *galantuomini*. The teacher, the local surveyor, the judge, chief of police — all kinds of regional and governmental officials belong also to this group. Included in this class also were businessmen such as agents, middleman and of course, the *gabelotto* (agent). The inclusion in this class of such diversified elements is further proof of the absence of a genuine middle class and it also denotes the segregation of the peasants and other artisans from all other members of the town population. (97)

The unifying factor of the *galantuomo* class was not "blue blood" of the nobility but rather the recognition of a significant cultural difference between them and the other classes. The wealthier members of the *galantuomo* class, such as the large landowners, were quite skilled at utilizing local government to serve their own financial gains. The other members of the *galantuomo* class, such as the doctor, lawyer, teacher, or notary, often did little to counteract the power of the landowners, and often took a passive attitude toward the almost intolerable living conditions of the peasants. Like the entire population of a town, these men were dependent upon the landowner for their economic security.

The incomes of the professionals, the doctor, lawyer, and the teacher, were rather insufficient. The teacher, at the lowest economic level, rarely made a salary of over 750 lire, or $150. These men were often landowners themselves and rented out small parcels of land to the *contadini* as a way to augment their income. Regardless of whether an individual was a landowner, professional, or government official, they were addressed by the hereditary title of *Don* or *Donna*.

The *speziale*, or apothecary, occupied a special place within the ranks of the *galantuomo* class. His profession retained the ancient attributes of dignity and respect. Usually trained at a university, the *speziale* was usually an elderly man honored for his responsibility to and local knowledge of the local community. Covello says that the *speziale*'s shop became a club for the elite. "The wine shop and barber shop were meeting places of the better elements of the town, but here were found the young or empty-headed, or merely the thirsty. The druggist shop was the center of the leisured class, the rendezvous of the philosophers" (Covello, 100).

Based on Covello's description of the *galantuomo* class and family history, it is quite possible that the Sgritta family were members of this class. However, it is believed that because family income substantially dwindled over the decades, it became necessary for the men to acquire artisan trades. Dominic was, in fact, the supervisor of a mill in Salerno, and as such, probably did not do too much in the way of manual labor (See Figure 1). His sons, however, were trained in the artisan trades of carpentry and masonry.

Whether it was to escape invaders and conquerors or the threat of malaria from the lowland swamps, most cities and towns in Southern Italy were built on steep mountain slopes or high on top of the mountains. Clusters of cube shaped houses spilled down the hillsides. "The architecture's rugged uniformity of style, identical color of the buildings clustered together, scarcity of trees and a conspicuous absence of high protruding chimneys, gave such towns the appearance of castle fortifications, rather than residential centers" (Covello, 67).

Each town had a *piazza (chiazza)* usually with a church at one end and the local wineshop at the other. The piazza was not only the marketplace, but also the emotional and social center of the town. The climate of the South was the sort of climate that permitted people to live out of doors. Mangione believes that it was this climate that gave character to the piazza:

> Everything was out in the open, yet subtleties had to be found to hide feelings. People seemed to speak louder because of this outside living. One often felt on a stage, aware that one was being observed, watched. On those summer nights, when the light lingered, the *chiazza* took on the dramatic air of a stage with many entrances. (Mangione, 36)

Social rules and rituals strictly governed the evening promenade. Arm in arm, the men of the town would walk in groups of two or three from one end of the square to the other. One's partner or partners was chosen from one's rank and status within the community. In other words, truckers would walk with other truckers or miners, artisans with other artisans or shopkeepers, priests with priests, or other members of the bourgeoisie. They would stop, chat for a while, glance about at the others, and start back for the other side of the square, often stopping at the cafe owned by generations of the same family. The men would nod in greeting to the members of their own station. A woman was only greeted if she was accompanied by her husband because "a man could be made cuckold by a glance" (36). Here, too, mothers walked with their marriageable daughters to the church, and home again.

Throughout the town, the streets were interrupted by smaller courtyards called *cortile*. Six or eight houses surrounded each cortile. Although the *cortile* theoretically belonged to the town, the residents would often turned it into a private central courtyard by putting a door or gate across its entrance. Although almost all houses were built exclusively of stone, the style of the house easily identified the class and circumstances of its owner. A one-story home, on average, costs about 500 lire, including the land on which it was built. A two-story home cost between 700 to 1,000 lire. Because these sums of money were quite out of reach for the peasant, he often could not afford to own a house.

Most *contadini* lived in single-story huts. Entrance to the living quarters was directly from the street. The ground floor was used to house the *contadini*'s animals, while the family's sleeping quarters were crowded into a loft reached by using a crude ladder. If the house had two rooms, the animals were separated from the family. But even if there was only one room, the animals were given shelter in it. Because there were no windows, the front door was usually left open to let in the light. If there were a second floor, only one window would be facing the front. There was rarely a back door or a back window.

Donna Gabaccia, in her work *From Sicily to Elizabeth Street* describes the typical home of the *contadini* as follows:

> Most simple agrotown houses were of stone and quite small, measuring upwards from ten to twelve feet square. Each had a dirt, or, at best, a brick floor, whitewashed interior walls unbroken by windows, and a cane ceiling beneath a tiled roof. The hearth was a large flat stone or a simple stove called a *focularu*. A loft at the rear of the room created an alcove. (18)

Light was provided by kerosene lamps. Most homes had ovens, but the poor cooked outside on stone piles fueled with straw or twigs. Because of the great deal of smoke from inside cooking and inadequate ventilation, the soot covering the walls of the peasant household gave it a grim appearance. Little could be done to remedy this situation, and the peasants considered it a useless waste of time, money, and labor. "A newly whitewashed house was usually the sign of some extraordinary event in the household, such as a wedding or a baptism. Few other events would move the peasant to whiten the blackened walls of his residence" (Covello, 75).

For many of the rich, as well as the poor, plumbing did not become popular until the twentieth century. Sewers were unknown except in the big cities. There were no cesspools in rural towns, and the use of outdoor toilets, even among the peasants, was uncommon. In some villages, a specific area was designated as a public toilet for children and men. In others, urinals and chamber pots were emptied into the streets. There was little initiative on the part of local leaders to improve public hygiene, and the national government did not make provisions for health or sanitation. Although the areas where the *galantuomini* lived were kept fairly clean, the peasant sections of town were not. There was no pavement of any kind and no sidewalk. Instead of streets, a series of stone steps were used by both people and animals to climb the mountain slopes. Where there were streets, they were narrow and cobblestoned, and needed of repair. The places where the cobblestones were missing were filled with water or debris.[5]

The better social standing of the artisan class was evident from the fact that he lived in a better house than the *contadino*. Typically, a two-story structure, the artisan or storekeeper used the ground floor to house his animals and for his workshop or store. The second floor was reserved for family use only. This type of house had plenty of windows, tiled floors, plastered ceilings, and walls. In place of the *focularu*, there was often a tiled stove and oven. Almost half of these homes contained five to nine rooms (Gabaccia, 20).

The homes of the aristocrats, professionals, government officials, and large landowner were called palazzos or *casa civile*. Far larger and grander than the homes of the lower classes, the *casa civile* had as few as ten rooms and as many as thirty rooms. Other comforts included pit toilets and a private well, balconies and terraces, and a private courtyard. The courtyard was closed to the street by a large door called a *porte-cochere*. Although many of the towns of southern Italy lacked the facilities and comforts of a "contemporaneous European civilization" (Covello, 72), the areas in which the upper classes lived reflected wealth and knowledge of North Italian living standards.

---

[5] See Covello: "The outward sordidness of the peasant section of the town was, however, in sharp contrast to the appearance of the inside of the home of the tenant. Despite a lack of space; despite the comparative primitiveness of the peasant household; despite even the need to house invaluable farm animals, an unexpected cleanliness and orderliness prevailed in most of the peasant homes" (75).

No matter how big or small, what was of the utmost importance to the Southern Italian was a house. "As little as it is, so long as it's mine" (Gabaccia, 13). A house on the second floor, or *casa di susu*, was preferred over a ground floor house, a *casa di jusu*, because it was away from the curious eyes of the neighbors. "One never knows what will come raining down on one's head from above." The second floor was called the *piano nobile.* A house with plenty of sunlight was also valued because "dark houses bring the doctor" (13). While a large house with many rooms was ideal, the Southern Italians also believed the house should be appropriate for its inhabitants, "a little nest for a little bird" (13). Above all, parents wanted their children to continue to live close by after they married. These housing patterns would be reflected in the choices made by the Sgritta family in selecting their homes.

LA VIA VECCHIA: THE FAMILY

The division between public and private space became essential to the Southern Italian family at the end of the nineteenth century. A house was any space that was occupied or owned by a household. "Just as eating together or sleeping together formed the functional boundaries around the household, the room or rooms used for these purposes divided the private center of the house from other, more public spaces" (Gabaccia, 29). Private space, therefore, was defined as any space that was accessible to the members of the nuclear family household. Family members, as they moved from town, to cortile, to house "recognized the physical separation of the world into distinctive spheres, each with its own rules for human behavior" (Gabaccia, 30).

The wealthy Southern Italians made the second-floor rooms in their homes their private spaces. These rooms were distinctly separate from the ground floor where the storage rooms and animal stalls were located, as well as from second floor rooms where servants might work or outsiders, "guests," could be entertained. "The decoration of the private quarters and the more public receiving room *(salotto)* further emphasized the boundary. The *salotto* became a room for secular display" (29). The rooms often contained imported pianos and heavy wood furniture. Popular were wooden cabinets with glass doors holding a display of ceramics, glass items, coffee pots, and travel mementoes. "Private rooms, by contrast, held simple furnishings. Religious prints and embroidered bedding excepted, they also remained quite unadorned" (Gabaccia, *From Sicily to Elizabeth Street*, 30).

Artisans and merchants, as well as wealthier peasants, were able to duplicate the segregation of private eating and sleeping areas in their smaller homes. The ground floor was occupied by the artisan workshops or merchants' sales room, as well as storage areas. The family lived upstairs on the *piano nobile*. Although less prosperous than the *civili*, these families attempted to create a *salotto* there. They filled the *salotto* with as many straight backed locally made chairs as they could afford, and a chiffonier also might complete the decor. Depending on the number of rooms available, the family might divide the space into private sleeping rooms, a living/eating room *(soggiorno),* and a kitchen. "Their large-doored and many-windowed houses symbolized not a threat to family privacy but the achievement of housing ideals" (Gabaccia, 49).

Peasant families, however, faced the impossible task of keeping private and public spaces separate. Donna Gabaccia believes that the privacy of family life was to the peasant," an important symbol of their solidarity in competition with others" (Gabaccia, 45). Yet Gabaccia continues, "within a single room or two families also carved out certain functional areas" (45).

The alcove that was formed by the loft at the rear of the house became the parents' sleeping area. The sons slept above in the loft while the daughters slept in the main room at night. Both sleeping and eating areas were decorated with religiously significant objects, such as pictures or calendars depicting saints, palm branches, etc. However, because much of the time the front door was open to let in the light, "a passerby, the women in the cortile, or a caller could easily check the condition of the bed linen, the amount of grain stored in the corner, the absence of household goods, or the dirt floor" (Gabaccia, 44). Peasants could not offer hospitality in their homes without exposing their private space.

Regardless of its size or amenities, the house was, for the Southern Italian, the focus of family identification. The word *casa* is used not only to describe the physical dwelling but also the closest of kin. Gabaccia comments that "the house, inseparable linguistically or conceptually from the family, physically served the family's idealized withdrawal into itself from the competitive world outside, somewhat as it did in Victorian America or in working class American more recently" (Gabaccia, 32).

The most important system to the people of the *Mezzogiorno* was the unwritten, but all-demanding *l'ordine della famiglia,* the rules that governed one's relationship within the family, one's responsibility to the family, and one's position within the family.

It is essential to understand this aspect of Italian social culture because it continues to dictate appropriate social behavior for both men and women in the United States.

Richard Gambino describes these complex social relationships in his book *Blood of My Blood.* He says that there are four different types of relationships governed by *l'ordine della famiglia*. The first is, above all, family members. This included one's blood relatives, including very distant members, cousins, aunts, and uncles. The second relationship is in which selected outsiders become important extended family members through the practice of *comparaggio,* or godparenthood. *Compari* and *padrini,* and their female equivalents, *commare* and *madrine,* were not necessarily godparents within the rites of the Catholic Church. They could better be described as intimate friends or respected elders. Third, there were *amici* or *amici di cappello* (friends to which one would tip one's hat), meaning those whose family honor dictated respect. The term *stranieri,* or strangers, was used for all others that one might speak to during the course of the day, people one worked with, shop owners, etc.

Since the status of *padrini* and *madrine* and *compari* and *commare* were the most essential designations in relationships after blood relatives, the choosing of those outsiders who would be admitted to the family circle was done with care. Couples put a great deal of thought into who they would choose to "stand up" for them at their weddings as maid of honor or best man, or who be chosen to be godparents for their children. The couples who made the selection and those chosen would thereafter call each other *commare* and compare. Godparents were greatly respected and were often addressed as *zia* (aunt) or *zio* (uncle). They were consulted when decisions were made, and their advice was accepted. However, in any conflict between blood and godparents, the blood came first. This ritual of *compareggio* played an important role in extending the family's network in the New World.

The development of relationships with people outside the family became deeply ritualized and steadfast rules were followed. An ironclad rule was that one had nothing to do with *stranieri*. One had to go up the hierarchy from the classification of stranger to friendly acquaintance before any human discourse could begin. "In a curious psychological twist of logic, the rule was observed by permitting passage from one class to the next highest through the rite of sharing a meal (or just coffee), a symbolic entering into the ceremony of family communion" (Gambino, 27). Being invited to be one's intimate was one of the greatest honors, and to refuse was a great insult.

> Usually, the two people involved gradually became more intimate in their conversations through degrees of codified, circumspect conversation. If one accepted the gambit offered by the other, then one or the other would move to the next degree. If the gambit was refused, the relationship went no

deeper and its progress stopped well short of the point of an honor offered and refused (29).

The nuclear family was the basic unit of Southern Italian life. Richard Gambino, in his book *Blood of My Blood*, comments about the family patterns of Southern Italy:

> The unique family pattern of Southern Italy constituted the real sovereignty of that land, regardless of which governments nominally ruled it. Governments and aliens came and went over the centuries. If they brought any customs that might strengthen the family system, these were gradually absorbed. But those customs that were hostile to the family were resisted. (5)

The members of the household ate together and slept together. People from other households were deliberately and rigorously excluded from the family's private quarters. A woman named Charlotte Chapman, who was conducting fieldwork in Milocca, Sicily, found it difficult to find a family that would rent her a room. No one wanted to take on the responsibility for the conduct of a stranger, an unattached female at that, by making her a part of their household. Although Chapman finally found a place to stay, she became quickly aware that the Southern Italians had no concept of boarding. "As one who remained outside the nuclear family circle of economic cooperation, she could not join the family at the table except as an invited guest on grand occasions. She received her cooked meal separately, eating alone in her rented room" (Gabaccia, 28).

Within the marriage unit, the father's position as *capo di famiglia* was firmly established and was unquestioned by other family members. He represented the family and its honor and prestige to the village and community. Gambino comments on the role of the father as follows:

> The father, as the ultimate retainer of la via vecchia, made all important decisions concerning the family. A living for the family and good marriages for its children were the primary goals toward which decisions were aimed. In this culture, young people had to re-establish in each generation the only social reality of the land, the family, by marriage. Therefore, a good marriage was more than just a question of social status. It was tantamount to survival and was treated as a basic bread-and-butter necessity. (7)

The father's rule as *capo di famiglia* was dependent on many factors. His prestige within the family was not by father-right alone. Factors such as his health, age, and ability to work and provide for his family also came into play. As long as the father was virile, he retained the title of *capo di famiglia*. None of the children, even the older and married ones, would challenge his authority. To oppose the authority of a father was conduct considered to be in bad taste. When the father began to show signs of weakness, however, a new *capo* would appear among the older sons of the family. The father continued to retain the respect of his children, but there was no longer blind obedience.

Leonard Covello says that the tradition of the older son assuming the role of *capo di famiglia* is significant.

> With the older son assuming the duties of head of household and remaining in the home of his parents, the bond of family solidarity were less disturbed than when the parents established their domicile in the home of a less important relative. The parental roof served as a symbol to perpetuate the "onore di famiglia" whereas the removal of the family seat to another household had a weakening effect upon the unity of the family. (195)

Gambino says if the father is the monarch in the family kingdom, the mother was the powerful minister of internal affairs. She was not only the emotional center of her immediate family but was also an important contributor to the family's economy. The father played a passive role in the family's internal affairs, reserving veto power only when things were being mismanaged. The wife and mother played a dominant role in home production and controlled the family's purse. She was responsible for finding suitable matches for her children. It was only after the match had been quietly and carefully arranged by the mothers, aunts, and godmothers of the young couple, that the fathers would become involved in the negotiations. A mother was also responsible for ensuring that her children were *ben educati.* "This notion of being well educated had nothing to do with schooling. Rather, it meant being brought up to value *la via vecchia* in thought and feeling, and to honor it in practice" (Gambino, 8). The status of a mother did not change upon her children's marriage. As will be seen in later discussions, as we will see in the case of Angelina Sorrentino, the traditional roles of the Italian mother would remain with her, even across the ocean.

The people of the *Mezzogiorno* saw the death of the mother as the ultimate disaster. The importance of the mother to the family is reflected in an Italian proverb that says, "If a father is dead, the family suffers; if a mother dies, the family cannot exist" (Covello, 208). A replacement for the father could be easily found by the assumption of the oldest son of the responsibilities and duties of *capo di famiglia*. It was difficult, however, to find a new center. A new woman coming into the home as a mother would mean more children. She would either bring them from a former marriage, if a widow, or bear them if marrying for the first time as a young girl" (Gambino, 27).

A woman's status changed over time as she went from child to daughter to wife and finally to a mother. She was the center of the household, and although she was submissive to her husband outwardly, she had an absolute authority within her home. She did not, however, display it openly or seek public acknowledgment of it. Gambino says that this was accomplished "through an intricate pattern of interactions in which the famous female tactic, *'pigghiami cu bonu'* (stooping to conquer) played a major part" (5).

Leonard Covello and Richard Gambino share similar opinions regarding the importance of the mother's family within the marriage unit. Gambino says:

> In contrast to the apparent patriarchal image of *la famiglia*, the mother's family played an important part in her life after her marriage and in the lives of her children, especially in the formative young years. The maternal relatives formed the only insurance she had against the possibility of her husband's death. In the event of her widowhood while her oldest son was still a child, the responsibility for her welfare and that of her children would be assumed by her family, and not by her husband. (29)

Covello notes that in the case of a father's death, the widow is not supported by her husband's family, especially if children are involved. "The father's relatives showed themselves unwilling to assume the responsibility. It was, therefore, the woman's relatives who usually came to her aid" (Covello, 217). Covello further points out that although the death of a father was mourned because it was the removal of the *celmo della casa*, or the crossbeam of the house, the case of a mother's death caused "vociferous lamentations, chanting, and profound misery" (216). The customary lament was, "O, you cruel mother, you have forsaken us! How will we get along without the eyes of our mother to watch over us? Who will care for your children, who are now abandoned and orphans?" (216).

In the event of a mother's death, the care of the children was taken over by her family. Covello says that this separation of the children from the father after a mother's death signifies the deterioration of family ties. He quotes an old Italian from the district of Agrigento as saying:

> I cannot tell why it was so, but when a mother died the family usually fell apart. The small children were taken over to the mother's relatives, and the older ones felt that they could not live home anymore. So they moved — one to an uncle, another to an aunt, where they would help in all kind of work and earn their keep. When the father died and the mother remained alive the family always remained together like chickens around the hen. (217)

Since every member of the family unit played a role in the family's economy, it was not unusual, therefore, children were expected to contribute as soon as they were strong enough to do manual labor. The arrival of puberty was seen as the end of childhood and the beginning of responsibility. In southern Italy, boys usually began earning money at the age of 12, and girls began to do housework at the age of 10. As quoted in Gambino's book, an old Sicilian adage says, "When hair begins to grow between the legs, one is fit to work" (232). Covello comments, "in general, the children were inculcated with the idea that, with the advance of puberty, they were quite mature. Such a concept of maturity obviously left an imprint on the social outlook of the younger generation. The respect for work, however poor the returns might be, was instilled in the children. The parents considered the work habit of the young person not only in the light of economic gains but also in the light of training in discipline" (Covello, 230).

At seven, boys would begin their training to become contribute to the family economy. Sons of farmers began helping their fathers in the fields and sons of artisans would help in their fathers' shops. By twelve many boys were receiving a daily wage, and by the age of 14 many were journeymen, seeking employment throughout the countryside. Covello says that "the coming of age" for boys was of more social significance than that of a girl. At the age of maturity, that is, at the age when he assumed work, he was given other rights and responsibilities. "The boy would identify himself with the grown-up males. In some parts, he would be called compare (in the sense of equal), and the community would approvingly consider him as a member of his society" (Covello, 232). As a child, he would generally go around barefoot, except on special occasions when he would wear regular shoes made by the local shoemaker. Now, however, as a sign of reaching the age of young adulthood, a young man would wear *scarponi*, a type of moccasin that was the traditional footgear of the *contadino*. This signified that the boy was now doing a man's work.

With his entrance into young adulthood, the boy was also given certain rights within the family unit. Although he had always been instructed in a man's priority over a woman, he was now given the opportunity to exercise this importance. If he was the oldest son, then he was given uncompromising priority over all his siblings. One Italian is quoted as saying:

> My uncle was the dominant character in his family and was assisted by his oldest son, who at the time, was about thirteen years old. This boy had the privilege of telling the other brothers and sisters what to do and what not to do. Naturally, everybody obeyed the parents, but the dominant person was the oldest boy, especially at times when the other brothers and sisters were recalcitrant. Whenever we went to the uncle's house the boy would

boss us too, for the uncle was the head of the family and we children were younger than this thirteen-year-old cousin of ours. (Covello, 232)

A boy's reaching the age of maturity gave him, as Covello says, "an openly recognized right to dominate his sisters, and simultaneously, placed upon him a responsibility for their conduct" (232). He used this role as guardian over his sisters with the utmost intensity. The sisters did not question the dominance of their brother. Often, this submissiveness was motivated by fear. One Italian woman comments:

There is no doubt we were afraid of our brothers more than of our father. The father may have been severe at times, but at other times he could be lenient. But never our brothers. They went after the least slip we made. They were, to us girls, anything but kind. (Covello, 233)

Another woman says that she had dual feelings for her brothers:

When I needed protection from a fresh boy in our village, or when someone made a remark about my legs and I felt like crying, it was the brothers to whom I went for help. I would also expect help from my parents. But when I was in trouble and it was my own fault, I avoided my brothers for fear that they would beat me. In those cases, I rather confided in my mother, seeking her protection against my brothers. (233)

Covello stresses that the authority of an Italian mother can be demonstrated quite clearly in how a brother treats his sister at home. It appears that the boy had two patterns of behavior, one displayed in the presence of the father and the other in the mother's presence. He says, "The implication was that the inculcation of a boy's attitude of superiority as a male was principally the product of paternal influence" (233). A mother's presence frequently blunted her son's attitude towards her daughters. An elderly Italian man remembers:

> I admit that I try to boss my sister; but not when my mother is around. On those occasions I often take orders from my sister. I help her dry the dishes, clean the house, etc. My mother would not stand for my ordering my sister around. And you know she is after all, my mother. (Here the narrator shrugged his shoulders, indicating that the mother's authority is inviolable.) But when my father is around, the situation changes not so much in deeds as in attitude. When my father is around, I become domineering over my sister. At times my father wins; more often, however, mother prevails. (236)

A young girl was left under the supervision of her mother. Training in the household's skills of cooking, baking, laundering, sewing, and taking care of the younger children, was seen as preparation for her future role of wife and mother. Covello says that popular tradition demanded that a girl not be idle. A proverb from Messina, Sicily says "*Le figghiole pultrune non acchiappanu mariti* (Lazy girls do not catch husbands)." A girl was also taught to accept the domination of all males, including her future husband. In her home she was expected to respect her brothers, even if they might be younger. Covello says that in parallel with this inculcation of submissiveness, a mother would also teach her daughter how to assert herself in her dealings with men. *Pigghiari cu bonu* — the art of diplomatic approach to men, a form of 'stooping to conquer' — was never overlooked by the mother and openly taught to the daughter" (Covello, 231).

As in the case with the boys, when girls became actively working members of the family, they acquired a social status within the family, as well as in the community. In Sicily once a girl has stopped playing with her dolls, she was no longer called a *picciridda* (girl) but instead *cummaredda* (little godmother). A symbol of her initiation into adulthood was the shawl she was given the privilege to wear. Instead of braids, she would wear the same hairstyle as the other women. She was allowed to mingle with the other women at the public fountain, go with them to the river to do the laundry and participate in the women's songs and the gossip of the neighbors. In turn, however, she was expected to act with dignity. Running or jumping were now behaviors in bad taste. Married daughters were expected to be obedient to their husbands, thrifty housewives and raise large families. When a young wife moved into the home of her husband's family, she was expected to take over the bulk of the household work. However, she remained subservient to her mother-in-law. Daughters still felt obligated to their parents and would help them with either money or labor (Ewen, 35).

Although work was an essential aspect in the lives of Southern Italian children, school was not. Italian laws mandated that all children, boys, and girls between the ages of six and nine, attend school. Many schools were poorly financed and badly organized, and attendance laws were not enforced in many areas. If a child went to a public school, it was probable that he or she would only receive an education in the early primary grades. In privately run church schools, most often attended by children of wealthier families, girls were sent to learn fancy embroidery and dressmaking. There were very few high schools in the south and they were largely attended by boys seeking technical training. As late as 1907-1908 statistics compiled by the Italian government indicate that only 20 percent of children were enrolled in school, which was the equivalent to grades one to three in the United States (Cohen, 22). Of all the classes in Italian society, it was the artisans who took the most advantage of the country's educational system.

Dominic had insisted that all his children go to

school and learn a trade. Carlo, however, never went to school. He would often come home with the buttons missing from his pants. Then his parents would know that he was playing with the boys instead of going to school. The children would take the buttons off their pants and flip them like pennies, playing for prizes of nuts.

According to Elizabeth Ewen, the family system "bound parents and children into a system of mutual obligation" (39). Fathers taught their sons how to work the land or a trade, while mothers prepared their daughters the skills necessary to run their own households. Through inheritance and dowries parents enable their children to create families of their own. However, children were expected to support their parents in their old age. It was considered a breach of family tradition to transfer a parent to a home for the aged, or to even permit them to live with others.

The ambition of every mother was to see all her daughters *sistemate* or settled before her death. Marriage occured at an early age, girls often as young as 14 and boys only a few years older. Sisters within a family were married in turn according to their age. Traditionally, parents would select the appropriate spouses for their children. Gambino says that marriage was looked on in the *Mezzogiorno* as first an alliance of families, and only secondary as a union of individuals. As such each family was required to contribute equally to the compact. Often the services of an *ambasciatrice* (emissary) were used to arrange the details of the match. The *ambasciatrice* was usually an older woman who had no relationship with either family.

Phyllis Williams, in her classic handbook for social workers called *South Italian Folkways in Europe and America*, says that while in theory a girl had little choice in the selection of her husband, she sometimes succeeded in picking the candidate and was seldom coerced into a marriage with someone she disliked. "When a girl became interested in some particular man, she could always confide in her godmother, who usually stood closer to her than her own mother. If she approved of the man, the godmother then went to his mother, who was presumably on the lookout for a suitable wife for her son" (Williams, 83). If the goddaughter was accepted as a candidate by the man's mother, then the parents were brought into the matter and a dowry discussed. When all parties were satisfied, the matter was settled.

The bride's family announced the young couple's engagement at a large feast or family gathering. Williams says that traditionally the prospective groom was allowed to see his betrothed only three times between this meeting and the marriage. And this literally meant seeing because he was not allowed to touch or kiss her. Some Italian women told Williams, "Kissing is an American custom" (84).

Gambino says that "traditional *contadino* society, encouraged passionate courtship feelings, yet greatly restricted courtship behavior" (Gambino, 187). In the early stages of their engagement, most of the communication between the young couples was through their chaperones. Later, they were able to talk together directly. However, they remained within earshot of their chaperones. As time passed, they were permitted to speak privately together, but always within the sight of the chaperones. Through the constant supervision by chaperones, their parents approved expressions of love between the two young people. Gambino says that this license was extended to engaged people only. "A man who declared his love or passions without this license would seriously offend the woman's family. A woman who approached a man without the license would disgrace herself and her family" (197). Although love was not considered necessary in a marriage, the young couple were encouraged to woo each other and speak of love to each other. The couples, however, were not permitted to hold hands or kiss, because in the *Mezzogiorno* people of the opposite sex, whether married or unmarried, did not touch each other in public.

Once the date for the wedding was set, preparations were made for the bride's dowry. Since a young girl had been planning for her marriage for years, the only thing that remained to be done was to make sure that the required number of sheets, towels and undergarments had been made. The extent of a trousseau was denoted by the expression *dodici e dodici* (twelve and twelve) or *venti e venti* (twenty and twenty). Williams says that many of these items were needed because of the lapse of time between family laundry. Never would the quantity be less than twelve, and any more than this number would indicate the elevated economic circumstances of the family. A husband was required to match the quantity of articles of clothing being furnished by his wife. For example, if she had twelve chemises, he would be required to have twelve shirts.

In most of southern Italy, the church ceremony had been the only legal form of marriage contract until 1870, when civil ceremonies took legal precedence. After the ceremony at the parish church, a feast was held in honor of the young couple. If a family could not afford it, the celebration of the event was held off until there was a special feast day. As the couple passed through the village, almond candy called *confetti* was thrown upon them. Since a wedding trip was generally too expensive, the bride and groom spent some seclusion in their new home or a different place provided by family or friends. Both Gambino and Williams mention the fact that it was the custom for the bride's mother and her mother-in-law to inspect the bed linens on the day after the marriage was consummated. Williams says that "in certain places, custom even required that a satisfactorily stained nuptial sheet be hung over the balcony or windowsill as a testimony of the girl's virtue" (82). The period that the bride and groom spent together was called *settimana della zita* (the bride's week). Gambino says that this was the time in which the groom was expected to pamper his bride (Gambino, *Blood of My Blood*, 199).

In nineteenth-century Italy the division of labor by men and women differed considerably from region to region. It is evident, however, that regardless of her social class, the Italian woman played a dominant role in the economic well-being of her family.

A woman's workday began before dawn when she would rise before her husband and get water for her family. Peasant women would have to go to the public fountain to fill their earthenware jugs. An artisan woman had water for the family's use delivered to her in the morning, either by a male water vendor or by a peasant woman who was paid to fetch it. If the family were prosperous, the wife would make coffee before the other family members hurried to their daily tasks.

Many of the daily household tasks performed by both peasant and artisan women were the same. They would dress and nurse the smaller children, clean the room or rooms where the family lived, and gather the ingredients for the family meals. Women of both classes relied on the talents of the local dressmaker or *maestra* to lay out the work for new clothes for them. This is, however, where the comparison stops.

The need for the peasant woman to earn extra money to supplement the family income often required her to leave her home. She might exchange or sell eggs to the more well-to-do families in town or do housework in the homes of wealthier women. Her small one-room home made a poor workplace even for more homebound tasks. There was little light and ventilation because there were no windows or chimneys. To compensate for this, however, most of her work was done outside in the cortile, with neighboring wives as her company. Women sat in their doorways making brooms, knitting, or spinning. On any one day, one or two women in the cortile would have to do laundry. Since not everyone owned a *pila* (washtub), borrowing was often done among one another.

An artisan wife who lived in a larger and lighter house had more control over where she chose to do her work. Most women preferred to do their work indoors and often chose the "best room" as their workplace. This room was the one that had the most windows in it. A bourgeoise housewife had a more varied supply of food and fuel, furniture, linens, clothes, pots, and dishes. She often benefited from household help hired from local peasant women looking to supplement their family incomes.

Women, in general, were in a better position than their husbands to make the right social connections and to find out about the reputations of other families. Donna Gabaccia comments, "a man's work companions were an ever-changing group of competitors with few resources beyond their own labor" (48). Although artisan and *civile* men were able to build large and complex social networks, peasant men were not able to "form reciprocal instrumental relations to others" (48). However, a woman's day-to-day tasks brought her into contact with more people of varying status. Gabaccia further says that the wives of the more prosperous landowners and artisans had less contact with her neighbors, while poor women met many through their daily chores. For the peasant woman, the women of the cortile were her constant companions, as they sat outside doing chores and supervising the children. "Village women's gossip passed along information about community members and also set standards and reinforced norms about proper behavior" (Cohen, 31). Even the poorest woman could, at one time or another, offer to help a neighbor with heavy household work, in caring for children, or during a family crisis. Gabaccia says, "if she did this for an artisan's wife, she gained a *padrona,* and she could expect a returned favor" (Gabaccia, 48), such as using a loom or a sewing machine. Many Italian husbands also acknowledged that their wives could handle a variety of tasks precisely because they were exposed to a more diverse group of people. "I'm alone in the fields all day. I have only the mule to talk to. What do I know about such things? My wife has more experience, go ask my wife" (Cohen, 32). Southern Italian women, therefore, earned a reputation as fast talkers and good arguers. They used these skills to their advantage in dealing with their husbands (in private, of course) and with other community members.

By the time Salvatore Sgritta married Candida Lanzare, sometime between 1896 and 1897, Italy was on the verge of economic collapse, agriculture was suffering from a severe depression, and the population was growing at an extremely high rate. An old Italian proverb says, *"Chi sta bene non si mouve"* or "He who is well off doesn't move." But at this time, the lives of many southern Italians, including the young Sgrittas, became difficult. For them and many others, immigration was the best and perhaps only way of improving their lives. Alexander DeConde, in his book, *Half Bitter, Half Sweet: An Excursion into Italian American History,* says that for Italians "their homeland virtually expelled them. They left in a mass act of protest against intolerable conditions" (DeConde, 97).

The Italian woman would take with her a few meager material possessions and all her Old-World traditions and customs. She would rely on the traditions of the Old Country to help her build a firm foundation for her family in the New World. There, she would remain the center of the family, continuing to nurture, contribute economically, and maintain the family's social networks. Miriam Cohen comments on the ability of the Italian women and the role that they would play as they joined their husbands in the United States:

> The heritage southern Italian women brought with them included their vital role in the family economy, epitomized by their hard work. In Italy

they were badly needed at home, and there was little opportunity for schooling, so young women stayed close at home. But Italian females, particularly married women, could not be excluded from the public world because the public and private realms were so closely intertwined. Navigating between public and private spheres would be different in New York and would provide new challenges. The women brought to America years of experience helping to manage household economic enterprises, juggling domestic chores, and raising children under difficult circumstances. In the United States they mustered these resources to deal with more years of hardship and struggle in a new land. (Cohen, 35-36)

LA VIA NUOVA

Salvatore Sgritta and his wife, Candida Lanzare, left their family and friends in Salerno, Italy and immigrated to the United States in October 1899 along with their infant son, Sabatino (See Figure 2). They were sponsored by Salvatore's brother, Alphonse, an inventor and had established a successful candle manufacturing business in Brooklyn, New York (See Figure 3). The ties of *famiglia* were even deeper between the two brothers because Alphonse was married to Candida's sister, Rosina. It is probable that the Sgrittas' first look at the United States was from Castle Garden because the buildings at Ellis Island had burnt down and were being rebuilt of non-flammable materials. Candida was pregnant when she left her homeland. The couple's second child, Angelina, was born in May 1900 in Manhattan.

It is possible that Salvatore was drawn to Stamford because he was a cabinetmaker by trade, and he was able to find work in one of the many furniture factories that were located there. At the turn of the century, Stamford was a bustling urban and manufacturing center. The train stopped at the Stamford railroad station every day since 1849 when the New York, New Haven, and Hartford railroad line was completed (Lobozza, 39). Stamford boasted an excellent harbor and at one time there had been direct trade with the West Indies. North of the city, in rural

Springdale, there were many large farms and quaint summer cottages for the wealthy and influential.

Vincenza (Jennie) Giovanna Sgritta, the third child of Candida and Salvatore, was born in Stamford on September 18, 1904 (See Figure 4). According to Jennie's birth certificate, the Sgritta family lived at 65 Pacific Street when she was born. It was a busy street of brick buildings that housed small shops and businesses on the ground floors and many immigrant families on the upper floors. There were anywhere from three to six families in a building. Each morning, Salvatore would walk to work at the Sleicher & Sons Piano Company, located at 484 Pacific Street. Candida stayed at home and cared for her three small children.

Salvatore was a well-educated man and could speak several languages. One of the first things he did when he came to the United States was to go to school at night to learn to read and write English. Jennie says that "sometime he would translate things for people who could not speak or read in English."[6] Eventually, he became an active union man and even the secretary of the carpenters union.

Tragically, in January 1906, Candida died suddenly from typhoid fever at the age of 27. Her death certificate indicates that she was only sick for about two weeks before she died. She was dressed for burial

---

[6] I cite from Jennie's *Memoirs of Jennie Sgritta,* her unpublished and hand-written autobiography, undated. The text was found among my grandmother's papers after her death. Among the collection are also the family papers of Grace Suppa.

by her friend, Mrs. Spina, and was laid out in the parlor where friends and neighbors could pay their respects. My grandmother was too young to remember any details about her mother's death. "My sister, Angelina, remembers someone picking her up to look in the casket," Jennie said. "'Look, there is your mother. Say good-bye to her'" (Calka-Norton 1995). The coffin was covered with a sheet of glass in an effort to keep the disease from spreading. Candida was buried in St. John's Cemetery, the new cemetery in the Springdale section of Stamford. Her grave was marked by a simple iron cross and remained that way until a stone was erected in her memory in 1930.

Salvatore needed someone to help him care for his children. He decided that Sabatino, who was seven years old, would stay with him. Angelina, only five years old, would go and live with her godparents, the Aievoles. As is the custom in Italy, when a mother dies, the Sgrittas turn to the Lanzare family for help. Carlo Sgritta, the third Sgritta son, brought little Jennie to Brooklyn to Alphonse and Rosina. The couple were financially comfortable and had two children: a son, Thomas, who was born in 1900, and a second child on the way (See Figure 4). Rosina adamantly refused to take the child. She was afraid that the typhoid disease would infect her family. So, Salvatore had to make other plans for his youngest child.

In Europe, Salvatore's parents, Dominic and Angelina, must have been worried about their son and their grandchildren. Dominic, a veteran of the Italian army, had retired from a good position as a mill foreman. He and his wife had raised a large family of five sons, Salvatore, Alphonse, Matteo, Carlo, and Dominic, who were now grown men. The couple had lost several daughters to disease during childhood. It is possible that Salvatore wrote to his mother for help. Although well into her sixties, Angelina was determined to go to America. On May 8, 1907, Angelina boarded the *S.S. Luisiana*, bound from Naples to New York (See Figure 5).[7]

There is not much known about Angelina's stay in America. We do know, using the City Directories for the town of Stamford for the years 1907 and 1908 as a reference, that both Salvatore and his brother Carlo were living at 24 Cove Road in 1907 and moved sometime in 1908 to Charter Street.[8] This might have been an effort to provide the family with more living space, which now, for the time being, includes Angelina. A family photograph was taken in Stamford quite soon after Angelina's arrival (See Figure 6.) Pictured in it were Angelina and her sons Salvatore and Carlo, her adopted daughter Anna, Jennie, and her older brother Sabatino. Jennie is standing between her grandmother and Anna. Looking at the picture from the aspect of body language alone, it is apparent that Jennie was more comfortable at this time with Anna than her grandmother. It is possible that Anna

---

[7] Ship Manifest, S. S. Luisiana, May 1907.
[8] Price and Lee Company, Stamford Directory (Stamford: Gillespie Brothers Printers, 1907 & 1908).

had been sent to the United States sometime in 1907 to marry Carlo, a marriage arranged by Angelina. If this is the case, the family had been living together under one roof, Anna becoming a mother figure for little Jennie.

My grandmother describes this event in her life in her memoirs as follows, "When I was two and one-half years old, my grandmother came from Italy. She stayed in this country for one and one-half years old. But my grandfather missed her too much. So, when the time came and she was going to leave, I was three and one-half years old and I didn't want my grandmother to go. Grandma said, 'I will bring her with me' (Sgritta Cerulli)." If Jennie's memory is accurate, then sometime towards the end of 1908 Angelina decided to return to Italy with little Jennie. It is interesting to note that on October 24, 1908, Salvatore was remarried to a young woman named Antoinette Leone. Could it have been that Angelina only stayed long enough to find another wife for her son?

Dominic and Angelina made a warm and loving home in Salerno for their grandchild. Dominic took a job as a doorman or "concierge" in a large luxury apartment building. There the family lived in a three-room flat had two bedrooms and a small parlor. Jennie and her grandmother slept in one bedroom and Dominic slept in the other. Jennie was her grandmother's constant companion.

There was a large brick fireplace in the backyard of the building. Here Jennie and her grandmother would boil laundry in a large kettle. The clean laundry would be brought to the roof, which it would be hung up to dry. "In the summertime," Jennie recalls, "when the grass was green and clean, we would lay the sheets in the sun to dry" (Calka-Norton 1995).

Meals were a family affair in the Sgritta home. Because they did not have any refrigeration, groceries had to be bought daily from the local market and food prepared "fresh." Jennie and her grandmother would bake their bread and cook in a tiny kitchen that they shared with other tenants in the building. Wine was served at each meal, ice cold from the cellar. My grandmother remembers that her grandparents had great affection for each other. Dominic would pour wine for his wife at each meal and toast her with "salute!"

My grandmother also remembers that her great-aunts, Dominic's sisters, would often visit them. In particular, she remembers Zia Katherine. Katherine always dressed like a lady, in fine dresses and fancy hats.[9] Jennie always wondered why this great-aunt never chewed her food but always seemed to let it melt in her mouth. She asked her grandmother, "Nonna, why does Zia Katherine eat her bread that way?" Her grandmother answered, "Because she doesn't have any teeth!" (Calka-Norton 1995).

---

[9] This may be further evidence that the Sgritta family had their origins within the aristocratic class because hats, in Italy, were reserved for the upper classes. The Sgrittas were thus more likely of the bourgeoisie class, who at this time were beginning to emulate the ways of the nobility. It is noteworthy that peasant women only wore scarves.

As a young child, Jennie had medical problems with her eyes and ears. Her grandmother would take her to the doctor, and he would say to the little girl, "Look at my forehead, Jennie." My grandmother vividly recalls that no matter how hard she tried to look at the doctor's forehead she couldn't. "The doctor wore shirts with big, starched cuffs," she said. "Every time he would tell me to look at his forehead, I would look down his sleeve instead. And every time I could see two little fleas dancing in his cuff" (Calka-Norton 1995).

Although Angelina had taken her granddaughter to many specialists in Salerno, no one could determine why the little girl could not see clearly. There was an old woman in town who offered to help. The old woman told Angelina to gather some moss that grew on the city's ancient walls, wash it thoroughly, and bring it to her. My grandmother said, "In the name of St. Lucy, the woman placed the moss under my eyelids. After that, I was able to see again" (Calka-Norton 1995).

Because Dominic was a staunch supporter of education for children, Jennie would also be required to go to school. A kindly old *cavaliere* who lived in the Sgrittas' apartment building offered to get her a place at the Institute Immaculate Concezione. This was a prestigious boarding school for young girls outside of Salerno that was run by an order of French nuns. There, my grandmother learned to read and write in Italian and Latin, to cook and sew, and to make fine embroideries and laces.

The little girls slept in dormitory style rooms with large windows. Each child had a trunk at the foot of her bed in which to keep her belongings. On balmy evenings the windows were left open to catch a cool breeze. "I can close my eyes now," said my grandmother, "and still remember the beautiful scent of orange blossoms filling our room" (Calka-Norton 1995). The Sisters were very frugal, and electricity was only used for a short while each night as the girls got ready for bed. If the little girls had to use the large, marble bathroom during the night, they had to walk in complete darkness. Because they were all frightened to walk in the dark alone, the girls would wake each other up and go together. My grandmother, who was as resourceful then as she was throughout her life, came up with a solution to the problem. She gathered together the leftover bits of embroidery thread and wax scrapings from the candles in the chapel and made candles for the girls to use.

In September of 1912, Jennie made her First Communion, an important rite of passage in the life of a young Catholic girl. Traditionally, children received this sacrament when reaching the age of 12. However, in August of 1910, Pope Pius X issued a papal decree called the *Quam Singulari Christus Amore*. It declared that children should receive First Communion as soon as they had acquired a basic knowledge of religion, typically at age seven (Perrot, 328). Jennie's communion dress was made from a dress she had brought with her from America, probably the same dress she had on in the 1908 Sgritta family portrait. The Sisters at the *Istituto lmmaculato Concezione* gave each little girl a white prayer book and a pair of white rosary beads. My grandmother remembers receiving holy cards with the date of her First Communion printed on the back. She posed for the traditional communion photograph with her grandfather. A copy of this picture was sent to her father in America. "My grandmother made sure that I wore my hair over my shoulder so that Papa would be surprised at how long it had become," recalled Jennie (Calka-Norton 1995; see Figure 7).

As the years passed, Lady Liberty continued to draw the Sgritta family to American shores. By 1913, all of the Sgritta children, with the exception of Matteo, had gone to live in the New York and Connecticut area. Dominic and Angelina were now 73 and 69, respectively. "My grandparents," said Jennie, "were concerned about what would happen to me if they died" (Calka-Norton 1995). The couple decided it was time to bring Jennie back to her father and join their sons in America. They booked passage aboard the *S.S. Giovanni*, which sailed from Naples on April 30, 1914.[10] Jennie and her grandmother shared a hard wooden bunk in the steerage section of the ship. Women would come around at mealtimes with soup for the young children. "My grandmother made sure that I got my share, each and every time," Jennie remembered (Calka-Norton 1995).

---

[10] Ship Manifest, S. S. Giovanni, 1914.

After 14 days at sea, the S. S. Giovanni pulled into New York Harbor. Jennie, because she was an American citizen, was separated from her grandparents at Ellis Island. She was brought to a separate room and given something to eat while she waited. "I kept crying for my grandparents," said Jennie. "Finally, a man brought me to them. Then my father was there to take us home" (Calka-Norton 1995).

As Jennie grew up in Italy, Salvatore began to make a new life in the United States. In 1908 (See Figure 8), he was remarried to a young woman, Antoinette Leone, who was ten years his junior. The 1910 Census, dated April 22, 1910, shows the couple living at 204 Charter Street with Salvatore's son, Sabatino (Bureau of the Census 1910).

Antoinette was from a large family of 14 children. Her mother died after the birth of her youngest sister, Mabel, while the family was still in Italy. Her father, John Leone, buried his wife and headed to America when Mabel was only two weeks old. John was a jeweler by trade, and although he had a large family, he must have been a man of some means. He buried his wife in a mausoleum and had a picture taken of it. This picture was hung on his bedroom wall and remained there until his death.

Salvatore and Antoinette had two children together. Their first child, a daughter, was born on May 5, 1910. She was to be named Madeline after her maternal grandmother. On the day of her christening, however, Salvatore decided to name the baby Candida after his first wife. I asked Candida why her mother allowed Salvatore to change her name. She said, "In those days, you just obeyed" (Calka-Norton 1996).

The couple's second child, Mattea, was born on August 12, 1912. Sadly, both Antoinette and the baby were to die in the winter of 1912. On December 4, 1912, Mattea died from infantile convulsions. Three weeks later, on December 20, 1912, Antoinette had a horrible accident. An article in *The Daily Advocate* from December 23, 1912, says that at approximately 9 p.m., Salvatore had gone across the street to see his brother. Antoinette had just put little Candida to bed and as she walked out of the room, the lighted kerosene lamp fell from her hands, igniting her clothing into flames. Salvatore saw the fire as he returned home and using dirt and water put out the fire. Antoinette, however, was severely burned on her face, neck, and right side. According to another newspaper article several days later, "Mrs. S'Gretti was taken with convulsions while carrying a lighted lamp, fell, and the lamp was broken. Her clothing caught fire, and she was badly burned before the fire was put out. Dr. James J. Costanzo, who attended her, entertained no hope for the woman from the first (*The Daily Advocate* 1912).

Candida was sent to live with her mother's family. John Leone and his daughters took good care of the little girl. Annie stayed at home while Rosie,

Susie and Mabel went out to work. Rosie and Mabel were sent to millinery school in New York City and later, they opened their own shop on West Main Street. Aunt Rosie also made bridal clothes, working for herself as well as for other shops. The aunts would fuss over Candy and make her pretty dresses and bows in her hair. My aunt remembers that her aunts would grow her hair long and would put her hair in rags to curl it for Sundays. "My brother," she said, "would get very angry. In the summertime he would make me cut my hair real short" (Calka-Norton 1996).

As Jennie settled into her new home on Avery Street, she had several adjustments to make. For one thing, she had a four-year-old sister, Candida, whom she had just met. This little sister was now Jennie's roommate and the two girls shared a big double bed. Jennie recalled this time of her life. She said, "My sister was surrounded with aunts, her mother's sisters. Each weekend she would go and stay with them. She would come home on Sunday with a new dress. I was sure some of the aunts did not like me" (Calka-Norton 1995). Candida remembers that "in the winter, it was cold in our house. There was only a coal stove in the basement to heat the rooms. So, Jennie would send me up to bed early to warm the bed. Then she would come in and put her cold feet on me!" The girls did not have flannel pajamas to wear, recalls Candida. "You just put on high wool stockings over your long johns" (Calka-Norton 1996).

The second obstacle my grandmother had was language. The principal at Cove School tried to place the 10-year-old in kindergarten! My grandmother was very indignant. She could speak and write in Latin and Italian. This little girl had studied at a fine girls' school in Italy. She didn't belong in kindergarten! She just didn't speak English. "The teacher finally put me in the third class," recalled Jennie (Calka-Norton 1996; see Figure 9).

The house on Avery Street was perfect for housing an extended family. It had three floors and was divided into two apartments. Angelina and Dominic lived in the first-floor apartment with Salvatore and his three children, Sabatino, Jennie, and Candida. The upstairs apartment was occupied by Anna, her husband, Michael Interlandi, and their children. At this time, Salvatore wanted his oldest daughter, Angelina, to come back and live with the family. Angelina had been taken in by her godparents, the Aeivoles, when her mother died in 1906. She was now a young woman of 16 and had no intention of leaving the people who had raised her. Salvatore tried to use legal action to force her to come back. Ultimately, he failed and had to be content with having all but one of his children back in the family nest (See Figure 10).

It was on Avery Street that Jennie began to learn about keeping a household from her grandmother. In her memoirs she wrote, "My grandmother began to teach me to bake bread and wash clothes in the style of those years" (Calka-Norton 1995). Although there was an icebox in the kitchen (Candida remembers that it was her job to ensure the drip pan was emptied), most things were bought fresh. During the week, Angelina would walk to the corner store for a small piece of meat. Once a week, Salvatore would go to the Italian grocer on Pacific Street and buy imported pasta in large wooden boxes and prunes and dried fruit. Angelina would dry apples in the sun in the fall. She would put apples and prunes in hot water on the stove. As the fruit cooked, she would have the children and her husband sit with her around the kitchen table and say the rosary. When the rosary was done, so was the fruit. Candida remembers that it was a delicious treat.

Angelina also planted a garden in the lot next to the Avery Street house. She planted pole beans on each side of the corn plants, as is the custom in the old country. The beans would be allowed to dry on the plant. On Sundays in the summer all the aunts would come over. The children's job was to shell the beans, which Angelina then stored in clean white flour bags. Dried sausage and salami were also part of the family's diet. They raised chickens for their eggs and meat and had rabbits as well. There was a rain barrel in the back yard which collected the water to wash the girls' hair.

When Angelina suffered a stroke a debilitating stroke in 1918, Candida, who was only eight years old, went back to live with her maternal grandfather and aunts. Jennie, as the oldest girl, took care of her invalid grandmother. On October 3, 1918, Angelina Sorrentino died from Spanish influenza at the age of 73. "We were all sick with the influenza when my grandmother died," remembered Jennie. "There were no automobiles at that time, just carriages. I remember looking out the window and watching the black funeral carriage with its plumed horses take my grandmother's coffin to the cemetery to be buried" (Calka-Norton 1996). Candida remembers that she did not see her grandmother "laid out" (Calka-Norton 1996). She had been the first in the Leone household to get the Spanish flu. Aunt Annie never got the flu and took care of them all. She treated their high fevers with cocoa quinine and nursed them back to health.

With the death of her grandmother, Jennie, at the young age of 14, became responsible for running the household. She had to do the cooking, cleaning and laundry for her father, her brother, her grandfather, and her little sister. It was at this time that Jennie left school.

My grandmother remembers that when she was 16 or 17 years old, one of her father's friends, Raphael Russo, had a son who wanted to "keep company" with her. Jennie said, "I told my father that I did not have any feelings for this boy. But he told me to take some time and that love would grow" (Calka-Norton 1995). Alphonse truly loved Jennie. He had his cousin come to her house and serenade her with his guitar. He brought her little gifts. But love did not grow for Jennie.

One Sunday afternoon, the two families got together at the Sgrittas' house to announce the engagement of the young people, a tradition carried over from *la via vecchia*. My grandmother remembers that there were benches lining the kitchen and parlor. "When Alphonse placed the engagement ring on my finger, I thought I was going to faint in front of all of those people" (Calka-Norton 1995). Love did not grow for Jennie, and, in the end, she broke off her engagement to Alphonse. Even after years had passed and Jennie had married my grandfather and Alphonse had found a wife, every time Alphonse's mother would meet Jennie's mother-in-law she would say, "You stole my girl from me!" (Calka-Norton 1995). Ironically, Raphael Russo is buried in the same row as his friend Salvatore Sgritta in St. John's Cemetery.

Jennie first met Giovanni (John) Cerulli on a Saturday afternoon in 1918 when she was 14. She was outside emptying the coal scuttle into the garden alongside the house. Her braids were a dark chestnut color and soot smeared her face. John had come to see her father. Without a second thought Jennie directed him upstairs to the family's apartment. Who would have dreamed this handsome young man would someday be Jennie's husband?

In 1922, however, the two young people met again. Candida recalls going to Mr. Truncone's house, a friend of her father's, who lived across the street from the Cerulli family on Stillwater Avenue. When the men played bocce, the two girls, Jennie and Candida, would walk arm and arm up and down the street. It is possible that this is when Jennie caught John's eye. This time, Jennie was also interested in the young man.

As was the tradition in the old country, John first approached Jennie's *Compare*, Dominic, and asked him for advice. It is possible that John will have thought that Jennie was still keeping company with Alphonse Russo. Dominic must have assured John that she was not, and then, in turn, must have asked Jennie about her feelings for John. Jennie, however, did not stand by the tradition of letting anyone be her go-between.

Letter writing was one of the major means of communication between my grandparents during their courtship. Their feelings for each other are seen in a series of letters and postcards they sent to one another between 1922 and 1923. It is evident that they had been in each other's company before, and a romance had developed from their casual acquaintance.

The only letter in Jennie's writing is the first letter, dated May 16, 1922. It must have held special significance for my grandfather because in it, Jennie tells him, "I want to let you know right well that I am not keeping company with anyone. I have had a date with someone, and my father knows all about it. I haven't told him anything at all now." Jennie may have wanted to "keep company" with John when she was matched to Alphonse by her father because she says,

"Very well, everything depended on me long ago and now depends on you." She encourages John's attention and tells him, "Don't take things too slow. My father is going to get married pretty soon, and I am going to go to work" (See Figure 11). Jennie also realizes that she was forward to write to John first. She says, "Please do not call me names or anything because I am writing to you and you, not to me. I know I am annoying you enough and excuse me if you have anything bad from me." In the letter's Postscript, she writes, "Excuse my writing because no one knows that I am writing to you but you" (Sgritta, letter to John Cerulli, May 16, 1922). John's reply to Jennie is dated May 18, 1922. He is happy to hear good news from her. He says, "I would like to see you and please tell me where I can see you. There is nothing for you to excuse because you have done me no wrong" (Cerulli, letter to Jennie Sgritta, May 18, 1922). In his letter dated May 22, 1922, John encourages Jennie to tell her father about the two of them. "Just a few lines to let you know to let me know if your father knows anything about us. Why don't you let him know and let me know what he says. Just tell him, that he is the son of so and so."

In John's letter of May 25, 1922, he tells Jennie that it is now up to her to let him know when her father is ready to see him. He also asks her what her thoughts are on the length of an engagement period. He writes, "I would want to ask you a question. If your father would say all right how much time would I have? I guess what I mean is I guess you remember when you told me to wait four years. I would like to wait the most about a couple of years. What do you say?"

By the end of May 1922, Jennie had told her father about her relationship with John. In his letter to Jennie, dated May 30, 1922, John says, "I am very glad to hear that your father knows that you are writing to me. Please let me know when you want me to come over when your father is ready." John tells her that he thought he would first come over by himself to be introduced, see what her father had to say, and then bring his father over at another time. But John is hopeful when he says, "You can tell your father and of course if he wants to see both of us at once please let me know. When you want to see me let me know both of us at once please let me know when you want to see me let me know the time and I will take a couple of hours off. The boss will let me go anytime."

By the end of the year, the two young people were engaged. (See Figures 12 and 13). As was the tradition from *la via vecchia,* Jennie began the preparation of her *trousseau*. Salvatore built a cedar chest for his daughter to hold all the things that she would need to begin a new household. Jennie's *Zia* Anna would help her with the sewing. Among the items included were several nightgowns with handmade lace, a set of handmade sheets decorated with handwoven angels, and a yellow silk bedspread. Rosina and Anna would represent the bride's family at the making of the bridal bed. According to tradition, it was bad luck for the bride to be the first one to make her bed. Instead, her female relatives would do the task with grand celebration. As each sheet, pillowcase, and comforter was added to the bed, the women would stop and make a toast to the newlywed. When the bed was finished, it was sprinkled with confetti candies for good luck.

Jennie was quite happy at the prospect of having a mother-in-law. The young girl had never known her own mother, and her grandmother, whom she had loved dearly, had also died. But Jennie's mother-in-law, Maria Grazia, was not a very kind person. She always needed to be in charge of everything and, at once, took over all the preparations for the wedding. Maria decided where Jennie would have her gown made, decided that the wedding dinner would be in her home, and she would prepare the menu and invite only certain guests. Jennie put up with it only because of an inborn respect for her elders. Jennie was allowed to choose her beaded headpiece, her beautiful veil with satin rosettes, and her handsome husband (See Figure 14). "I've told my daughter, Grace," my grandmother said, "that when I die, I want my headpiece and veil buried with me. It was the only thing my mother-in-law allowed me to choose" (Calka-Norton 1995). In January of 1996, when my grandmother passed away, we saw that her wishes were followed.

After the wedding reception and the newlyweds departed for their little apartment on Stephens Street,

Maria confronted Jennie's aunt, Rosina. In the tradition of the old country, she wanted Rosina to accompany her to the newlyweds' apartment on the following day and inspect the bed linens for signs of Jennie's virtue. Aunt Rosina stood up to Maria Grazia. "I would not treat my daughter with such embarrassment, and I will not do it to my niece," she said. When Maria Grazia arrived at the home of the newlyweds the next day, her son was equally indignant and refused to let his mother in, "So, you want me to raise the flag? Well, I won't do it!" (Calka-Norton 1995).

Like the majority of young Italian wives of her time, Jennie was pregnant with her first child only four months after she was married. The first child of Jennie Sgritta and Giovanni Cerulli, Vito, was born on December 1, 1924. Another child followed every two years — Salvatore, born in 1926; John, born in 1928; Grace, born in 1930; and Angelina, born in 1931. By the time Jennie was 27 years old, she had five small children under five years old. Regardless of her strict Roman Catholic upbringing, she became a proponent of birth control.

Salvatore was remarried in 1923 to Fiorina Ross. Fiorina had been Salvatore's sweetheart back in Salerno when she was 15 years old. Candida remembers her as a very cultured woman, who wore her hair in a bun and dressed in the long skirts of the old European style. She was quite talented and could sing beautifully in Italian. Fiorina had lived in Marseilles, France with her first husband and emigrated to the United

States when he died. A mutual friend of Salvatore's and Fiorina's told Salvatore that she had moved to Brooklyn. So, Salvatore hopped on the train and renewed his acquaintance with his old flame. Fiorina told Salvatore that in all her years she never expected to have his children call her mother! Of all Salvatore's marriages, this one would last the longest. The couple were married for 27 years until Fiorina's death in 1947.

Because Salvatore had a wife to maintain the family's household, Candida was left to pursue many things she wanted to do. At the age of 14 she left school and got her working papers. Candida wanted to be a hairdresser, but Salvatore wanted her to attend a clothing design school in New York. In the end, the headstrong young girl did neither. She took a job making suspenders. Within a short time, however, she took a job working for Mrs. Antonia Tamburri, finishing dresses and other clothing items. By the time she was 16, Candida had become proficient on the sewing machine.

Salvatore had many friends in Stamford who he had helped get their start when they first came to America. One of them was Dominic Iacuzio. Dominic boarded with the Sgritta family when he came to the United States in 1913, until he had saved enough money to have his wife and children join him in 1919. His wife, Rose, was family to the Sgrittas. Her sister, Mary, had married Salvatore's brother Dominic. The Iacuzio family settled on Euclid Street, one street over from Avery Street. Candida and Medio

Iacuzio were the same age and practically grew up together. As the children grew into young adults, so did their love grow. They were married in 1931 when Candida was 22 years old. The following year, their first child, Rose, was born. Candida's second child, Antoinette, however, was not born until 1941.

After a few brief years living with the Cerulli clan, Jennie and John moved into the upstairs apartment on Avery Street. By that time, Jennie had five small children. The additional help from her stepmother was gratefully welcomed. It was during this time that Dominic celebrated his ninetieth birthday. This was also the time during the Depression, and it was difficult for everyone to make ends meet. My grandmother managed to feed her children without going on welfare. A deep work ethic had been instilled in my grandfather's character. He would not take "charity." Instead, to earn money to feed his family, he worked for the WPCA on various projects in Stamford. Among them was the building of Cubetta Stadium for Stamford High School. Other food goods were grown in the garden on the spare lot on Avery Street, and the chickens provided eggs and meat.

By the 1940s Jennie and John's finances had grown enough to buy a home of their own. Located at 19 Clinton Avenue, the house was closer to John's parents than Jennie's. It was a large home with four bedrooms upstairs to accommodate the growing Cerulli family. In the backyard, John planted a rose garden for his wife. Jennie and John's children grew up, and by the 1950s, they began having their own families. My mother, Angelina Cerulli, married my father, John Calka, on June 7, 1953. I came into the Sgritta clan one year later, on August 26, 1954. My grandparents loved all their grandchildren, but I was special. My parents lived on Clinton Avenue with my grandparents when I was born. I was special to my grandfather because out of his thirteen grandchildren, I was the only one who "was born in his house."

In the 1960s, Jennie and John began taking foster children into their home. Even though their grandchildren visited regularly, the large house felt empty without any children. After John died in 1965, Jennie took in four Puerto Rican children, all from the same family. She did not want the state to split them into separate households, probably remembering how she felt as a child. Just like her grandmother, Jennie began raising children again when she was in her 60's. In the 1970s Jennie's foster sons were gone, and she spent her time volunteering at St. Joseph Hospital. In the 1980s she spent her time at the Salvation Army.

By the 1990s Jennie's health began to fail. After several hospital stays, Jennie died on January 9, 1996, in her ninety-second year.

Conclusion

In many instances it was necessary for an Italian woman to adapt to changes even before she boarded any ship to go to America. Mangione argues in *La Storia* that women were specially affected by family separation when their men left for America. Some even went into mourning. America was seen as a *mala femmina* (bad woman) who lured the men away from their families and made them forget. Especially disturbing was the leaving of a father, who always promised to return within a few years (Mangione, 92). If a wife did not hear from her husband for a period of time, she worried that he had found another woman. Husbands also worried about the fidelity of their wives. According to Maxine Schwartz Seller, "some southern Italian men left their marriages unconsummated before immigration. If their wives were unfaithful, they would know about it!" (Seller, 328).

The summons to join a husband in America was seen as a blessing or a disaster. To some wives, receiving a letter from their husbands to join them in America was a sign of love, and nothing had come between them. But to some women, such as Rosa Cavalieri, the summons to America was dreaded. She had been glad to be separated from her abusive husband, who had emigrated with several other men from her town. Needless to say, she was reluctant to follow him. Her mother, however, told her that she must go. "Yes, Rosa," she said, "you must go. However, bad that man is, he is your husband — he has the right to command you" (Ets, 160).

A woman was often confronted with many problems she was unprepared to cope with. "Within a short time, she was expected to obtain the documents and belongings she and her children needed for the voyage, sell whatever possessions there were, borrow money for the train fare, and do whatever else was necessary to make the journey possible" (Mangione, 93). Many women had never been out of their villages in their entire lives, nor had they ever dealt with government officials or moneylenders. If she could not find a friend or relative to help her, many women had to rely on the services of a subagent.

The reunion of husbands and wives at Ellis Island after long periods of separation was also stressful. Often, they did not even recognize each other. Sellers says:

> Conflicts were caused by differences in Americanization. A newly arrived wife was often shocked to find her husband so thoroughly Americanized in appearance, behavior, and values that she no longer felt comfortable with him. A wife whose appearance and behavior had been acceptable in the homeland might now seem drab, old-fashioned, and unattractive to the more Americanized husband. (119)

Other young women came to America to meet fiancées they had never met or hadn't seen in many years. Rosa relates the experiences of a young woman named Emilia, who was part of the group that emigrated with her from her hometown. She says, "The officer called the name again and let us pass. Then here came up a young man. He was dressed — O Madonna! — like the president of the United States! White gloves and a cane and a diamond pin in his tie" (Ets, 167). Emilia was so frightened she tried to run away. She did not recognize the young man as the Carlo she had known in the Old Country. And it is evident that Carlo was equally shocked to see Emilia. Rosa says, "He pulled her out from behind us and took her in his arms and kissed her. (In America a man can kiss the girl he is going to marry!) 'But I never thought you would come like this,' he said holding her off a little and looking at her headkerchief and full skirt" (167). In this case, however, the couple's reunion was a happy one. "'She looks just the same as when she was seven years old,' the young man said to Pep, and he was happy and laughing. "But I'm going to take her up Broad Street and buy her some American clothes before I take her home'" (167-168).

Candida Lanzare, unlike these two women, was fortunate to have emigrated as a family unit with her husband Salvatore, and her small son, Sabatino. She did not have these adjustments to make. Salvatore obtained the proper papers from the officials in Salerno, allowing the family to immigrate. He also made all the travel arrangements, including transportation to Naples, where they would embark on the ship to America. Candida did not have to worry that her clothes were old-fashioned. As a woman who was a member of the bourgeoisie class, she was well dressed, her clothing reflecting the European fashion of the day.

When Salvatore and Candida moved to Stamford, Candida faced a major adjustment. Gone was her support system of mothers, grandmothers, godmothers, sisters, and aunts, who provided a nurturing network for the children. Candida would now have to rely on other women who were not family but were likely to be neighbors who spoke her native language. Ewen says, "in a strange country immigrant women created a world within their own community" (39). She believes that women were barred from the larger culture by language, class, culture, or gender. Thus, women depended on each other. This relationship, says Ewen, "mediated the world of culture left behind and the alien culture they stepped into" (39).

Many pressures threatened the stability of Italian immigrant marriages in the New World. Immigration challenged this traditional arrangement by removing the couple from the supportive network of their family and friends, making new demands on them both as a couple and individuals and suggesting that there was a possibility of choice and change (Seller, 119). Families opened their doors to newly arrived families and kin and, in addition, took in boarders to supplement the family income. These two factors contributed to a lack of privacy and additional strain on marriages. The marriage of Carlo Sgritta and Anna Sabatini was adversely affected by the presence of a young boarder in their home, Michael Interlandi. Carlo's and Anna's marriage was an arranged marriage by Angelina Sorrentino, who wanted to tie her adopted daughter more permanently to the family. The couple's first child was born in December of 1908 when Anna was 18 years old. Family stories say that Anna fell in love with Michael Interlandi, and by 1910, Carlo and Anna were divorced. This may not have happened if Carlo and Anna had been surrounded by their family and community in the Old Country.

As far as housekeeping was concerned, Italian women were faced with a very large adjustment to make. A woman such as Candida Lanzare, who was used to the bourgeoisie way of life, did not have the advantage of having someone to help her with her chores. Angelina, however, had the advantage of Jennie and Candida in the home. She was able to train the young girls to do various simple tasks. Two activities that seem to typify the change are laundry and cooking. In the Old Country, doing the laundry was a social occasion. Women would gather in the open air and do their laundry in streams or in the cortile. In the United States, however, most women found the chore a drudgery. Although many apartments had the added convenience of direct access to cold water, hence the name "cold water" flat, women now confronted the chore alone. Angelina had a better time coping with the chores of cooking because she was able to grow many of the ingredients she needed, such as basil, tomatoes, zucchini, eggplants, and squash in the family garden. The rest of the Italian ingredients were obtained through frequent visits to the Italian grocer on Pacific Street.

The Sgritta women continued to exert much influence on their families, even after immigration to the United States. We can see that Angelina's role as mother, nurturer, and the center of the Sgritta family extended its way across the ocean to America, especially when Salvatore lost his young wife in 1906. It is also significant that she remained in the United States for almost two years, returning to Italy in 1908, only after being sure that her son was safely remarried.

The deaths of Candida Lanzare, Salvatore's first wife, and Antoinette Leone, his second wife, caused drastic fragmentation within the family. In the first case, the three small Sgritta children, Sabatino, Angelina, and Jennie, were split up among family members to be raised. Sabatino was the only one to remain with his father. In the second case, Candida went to live with her mother's family, both at the death of her mother, and in 1918, when her grandmother became severely ill. It is important to note that the children (except for Angelina) were not reunited again until 1914, when Angelina came from Italy and was able to anchor the family again.

When Jennie took over the household tasks of her grandmother, she, in fact, became the new center for the Sgritta family. It is significant that her father, Salvatore, did not remarry during this time because he had Jennie at home to take care of the household. He did remarry, however, when Jennie herself was to be married. Salvatore married his third wife, Fiorina Ross, in 1923, the same year Jennie married John Cerulli.

It is noteworthy that once Jennie's children were all grown, she became more individualistic in her interests. She had always liked caring for people and had wanted to be a nurse. So, during the 1950s she took a correspondence course and became an LPN. Her girls, Angelina and Grace, were expected to do the household chores. These duties remained theirs until well after they were married and had families of their own.

The idea of family history became extremely important to the middle-class family during the nineteenth century. Previously, the only legitimate family histories belonged to the aristocrats. Now, the middle-class family could create memories for themselves through the ritualization of daily life and the collection of trinkets and family memorabilia. A new medium called photography allowed families to freeze special events in time so those events could be relived repeatedly. People could develop real kinships for their families because they had a tangible way to remember them. The Sgritta family left a wealth of photographs that can be used as historical materials to analyze their story.

There are several facts that suggest that the Sgritta family considered family time and space more private than public. The very fact that Jennie's grandparents had slept in separate rooms indicates the privatization, even between men and women. The home was a place to be nurtured and be a safe haven. They ritualized family routines, which have left vivid memories over decades of time. Jennie remembers how her grandfather would affectionately toast his wife with wine at the family's evening meal. Marriage seemed to be open to consenting adults. Jennie did not have to marry Alphonse, even though he was the son of her father's friend. She was able to follow her heart and marry my grandfather. This openness to love contributed to an openness of equality in this marriage.

Religion greatly influenced the lives of this family. The Sgrittas were from Roman Catholic backgrounds and were very strong in their faith. The First Communion was a very significant event for Jennie. Jennie felt that her eyesight was cured because of an old woman's prayer to St. Lucy.

The state played little or no role in the lives of this family. The family was required to take care of its own. In Jennie's case, even though he was in his sixties, her grandfather got a job to support his family. The state did not give the old people any assistance, financial or otherwise.

The Sgrittas had a connection to an aristocratic past and emphasized education. Jennie's and Candida's great-great-great-grandfather had earned notoriety in the service of the King of Naples. Their grandfather, Dominic, was quite aware of his aristocratic status and insisted on a good education for his children.

The Sgritta and Leone families were nuclear families, where the fathers went out to work and the mothers stayed home to take care of their children. It is significant to note the negative effect of the death of the mother in these families. The death of Jennie's mother resulted in the separation of brothers and sisters for almost ten years because Salvatore had no one to take care of his children.

Conclusions can readily be drawn that the Sgritta family was not uprooted, as Oscar Handlin's peasants, but had made a conscious decision to immigrate to the United States. It is possible that at the turn of the century, the economic situation for the family of the bourgeoisie class was in a severe state. The family could not live in the manner in which they were accustomed. For the young Sgritta brothers, and later on their parents, the only way to improve their lifestyles was to move their family to America.

The Sgritta family was the type of family that Rudolph Vecoli describes in his critique of Handlin's *The Uprooted*. They were a cohesive kinship group where each member was responsible for advancing the family's welfare. Alphonse Sgritta, after becoming established in Manhattan in 1897, extended a helping hand to his brother Salvatore, who joined him with his family in 1899. In the following years, Salvatore sponsored his two younger brothers, Carlo and Dominic, and his elderly parents. The Sgritta brothers were not "birds of passage," as described in Kessner's work *The Golden Door*. This is evidenced by the very fact that they both immigrated with their wives, and they had planned, from the start, to make America their home.

Finally, I do not agree that the Sgritta family reflects the thesis of Humbert Nelli, who believes the sense of a cohesive. extended family was only a dream in Southern Italy, and only became a reality when Italians immigrated to the United States. I believe that the Sgrittas were a close-knit bourgeoisie family, where children were loved and nurtured. This sense of family was brought with them when they came to America.

When my grandmother, Jennie Sgritta, died on January 9, 1996, the disaster that results in the death of the mother in an Italian family became a painful reality to me. Although the family was greatly saddened by the loss of my grandfather in May 1965, the family remained intact. The large holiday gatherings may not have occurred at the old house on Clinton Avenue anymore, but the family gathered wherever Jennie was. And everyone was welcomed. The last time the family was together was at Jennie's funeral, and then, later, when the few treasures she had left were dispersed among the brothers and sisters, granddaughters, and grandsons.

Everyone in the Sgritta clan has mourned the death of Jennie. However, the loss has not been felt more deeply than in those remaining women. My mother and her sister feel the same uprootedness as I do. Jennie was our center, the one who gave us a sense of stability and security. She was the family peacemaker and wanted us to all get along — brother and sister, parent and child, husband and wife. Jennie nurtured us all with unconditional love and encouraging words of wisdom. As I continue to mourn for Jennie, a loss from which I will never recover, I also mourn the loss of the family of my childhood and the rootedness that an extended family has, with its natural ordering that comes from generations of responsibility to a set role in the family. But I am Jennie's legacy, and it is now my responsibility to see that the values and customs of *la via vecchia* are passed on to the children who come after me.

"I Dream of My Grandmother and Great Grandmother"
By Maria Mazziotti Gillan

I imagine them walking down rocky paths toward me,
strong Italian women returning
at dusk from fields where they worked all day on farms
built like steps up the sides
of steep mountains, graceful women carrying water in
terra-cotta jugs on their heads.

What I know of these women, whom I never met,
I know from my mother, a few pictures
of my grandmother, standing at the doorway of the
fieldstone house in Santo Mauro.
the stories my mother told of them,

but I know them most of all from watching my mother,
her strong arms lifting sheets out of the cold water in the
wringer washer, or from the way she stepped back,
wiping her hands on her homemade floursack apron,
and admired her jars of canned peaches
that glowed like amber in the dim cellar light.

I see those women in my mother
as she worked, grinning and happy,
in her garden that spilled its bounty into her arms.
She gave away baskets of peppers,
lettuce, eggplant, gave away bowls of pasta,
meatballs, zeppoli, loaves of homemade bread.
"It was a miracle," she said.
"The more I gave away, the more I had to give."

Now I see her in my daughter,
that same unending energy,
that quick mind,
that hand, open and extended to the world.
When I watch my daughter clean the kitchen counter,
watch her turn, laughing,

I remember my mother as she lay dying.
how she said of my daughter, "that Jennifer,
she's all the treasure you'll ever need."

I turn now, as my daughter turns,
and see my mother walking toward us
down crooked mountain paths,
behind her, all those women
dressed in black.

From *Things My Mother Told Me*. Toronto: Guernica, 1999. Originally published in *Voices in Italian Americana,* Volume 7.2 (1996). Reprinted here with the kind permission of Maria Mazziotti Gillan.

BIBLIOGRAPHY

Bureau of the Census, The Thirteenth Census of the United States: 1910 (published 1913).

Calka, Angelina. *Family Papers*. Unpublished.

Calka-Norton, Frances. *The Oral History of Vincenza Sgritta*. 1995. Unpublished paper for coursework at Sacred Heart University, "Princes to Peasants." Compiled from oral interviews conducted in Stamford, Connecticut with Jennie Sgritta Cerulli, February – March 1995.

Calka-Norton, Frances. Interview with Candida Sgritta Iacuzio. Stamford, Connecticut, September 1996.

Carano Donvito, Giovanni. *L'economia meridionale prima e dopo il Risorgimento*. Florence: Vallecchi, 1928.

Cohen, Miriam. *Workshop to Office: Two Generations of Italian Women in New York City 1900-1950*. Cambridge: UP, 1992.

Covello, Leonard. *The Social Background of the Italo-American School Child*. Totowa: Rowman & Littlefield, 1972.

DeConde, Alexander. *Half Bitter, Half Sweet: An Excursion into Italian American History*. New York: Scribner's Sons, 1971.

Dore, Grazia. "Some Social and Historical Aspects of Italian Emigration to America," *Journal of Social History*, I (Winter 1968).

Ets, Marie Hall. *Rosa: The Life of an Immigrant*, Minneapolis: U Minnesota P, 1970.

Ewen, Elizabeth. *Immigrant Women in the Land of Dollars: Life and Culture on the Lower East Side 1890-1925*. New York: Monthly Review Press, 1985.

Gabaccia, Donna R. *From Sicily to Elizabeth Street: Housing and Social Change Among Italian Immigrants 1880-1930*. Albany: SUNY Press, 1984.

Gambino, Richard. *Blood of My Blood: The Dilemma of the Italian Americans*. New York: Guernica, 1996.

Iorizzo, Luciano J. *The Italian Americans*. New York: Twayne Publishers, Inc., 1971.

Kessner, Thomas. *The Golden Door: Italian and Jewish Immigrant Mobility in New York City 1880-1915*. New York Oxford UP, 1977.

Kraut, Alan M. *The Huddled Masses: The Immigrant in American Society 1880- 1921*. Arlington Heights: Harlan Davidson, Inc., 1982.

Lobozza, Carl. *Stamford, Connecticut: Pictures from the Past*. Stamford: Stamford Historical Society, 1970.

Maglione, Connie A. and Carmen Anthony Fiore. *Voices of the Daughters*. Princeton: Townhouse Publishing, 1989.

Mangione, Jerre and Ben Morreale. *La Storia: Five Centuries of the Italian American Experience*. New York: Harper Collins, 1992.

Nelli, Humbert S. *From Immigrants to Ethics: The Italian Americans*. New York: Oxford UP, 1983.

Perrot, Michelle, ed., *History of Private Life: From the Fires of Revolution to the Great War*. Cambridge: Belknap Press, 1990.

Price and Lee Company, Stamford Directory. Stamford: Gillespie Brothers Printers, 1907 & 1908.

Rolle, Andrew. *The American Italians: Their History and culture*. Belmont: Wadsworth Publishing Company, 1972.

Seller, Maxine Schwartz, ed. *Immigrant Women*. Philadelphia: Temple UP, 1981.

Ship Manifest, S. S. Giovanni, 1914.

Ship Manifest, S.S. Luisiana, May 1907.

Vecoli, Rudolph. "Contadini in Chicago: A Critique of *The Uprooted*," *The Journal of American History* 51, December 1964.

Williams, Phyllis H. *South Italian Folkways in Europe and America*. New Haven: Yale UP, 1938.

Appendix A

Figure 1 – Domenic Sgritta

Figure 2 – Salvatore Sgritta and Candida Lanzare

Figure 3 – Alphonse and Rosina Sgritta

Figure 4 – Jennie Sgritta, August 1906

Figure 5 – Angelina Sorrentino

Figure 6 – Sgritta Family Portrait

Figure 7 – Jennie Sgritta's communion

Figure 8 – Salvatore Sgritta

Figure 9 – Jennie's class at Cove School

Figure 10 – Angelina Sgritta, 1915 ca.

Figure 11 – Jennie Sgritta and friend from work

Figure 12 – Jennie's engagement

Figure 13 – John Cerulli engagement

Figure 14 – John and Jennie's wedding

Figure 15 – Sgritta men

Appendix B

Sabatino Lanzare and Grace Albano
Parents of Candida and Rosina Lanzare

Vincenza Lauteri – Grandmother of Salvatore Sgritta

Angelina Sgritta, 21 years old

Angelina Sgritta and Lorenzo Merola, wedding

Emiddio Iacuzio – Stamford Special Police Officer

Candida Sgritta – 16 years old, circa 1926

Candida Sgritta and Sylvia Cerulli
Confirmation circa 1927

Candida Sgrita – Engagement Photo, circa 1931

Candida Sgritta Iacuzio – approx. 80 years old

Salvatore Sgritta and Children
Salvatore Sgritta's 90th Birthday

Salvatore Sgritta and grandchildren
Salvatore Sgritta's 90th Birthday

Salvatore Sgritta and great-grandchildren
Salvatore Sgritta's 90th Birthday

Sgritta Crest

Jennie Ognitta Verulli

I was born Sept 18 1904.

My mother past away at the age of 28 left 3 children. My father was a wonderfull man, cabinet maker and Carpenter.

My parents came in this country at age 26 married with one child. He went night school, and got a diploma. Some time he transelated for some one who could not speack English.

When I was 2 years old my grand mother came from Italy. she stayed this country for 1½. because my grandfather missed to much. So when time come she was going to leave. I was 3 years old. I didn't want my grandmother to go. Grandma said I will bring her with me. So I was there until I was 10 years all She capet me in school in a nuns school in which they teaches us children, neading sowing abrordrey. Wen my grandma and grandma talk it over. lets bring this grandaught back to her father. So when I went to school I quigly learn English I graduated from school. Mean time my grandmother teach me to backe bread wash close in the style of dose years.

Jennie's handwritten letter (p. 1)

my grandmother passed away and at 14 I had to do
every thing. cook, bake, wash, iron, so on,
I never went to work until I was 18 years old
Then my father married to a friend so I
went to work. I married at 19 years old.

Jennie's handwritten letter (p. 2)

INDEX OF NAMES

Avery Street 73-5, 84

Bonaparte, Napoleon 10-1
Bourbons 11, 13-5, 27,
Brooklyn 62, 64, 83,

Calka, John 85
Calka Cerulli, Angelina 96
Calka-Norton, Frances 64,
  67-77, 81-2, 99, 139
Carano Donvito, Giovanni
  23, 99
Cavalieri, Rosa 86
Cavour, Camillo Benso di 12
Cerulli, Giovanni (John) 77,
  79, 84, 92, 115, 116
Cerulli, Salvatore 82
Cerulli, Vito 82
Cerulli, Sylvia 127
Chapman, Charlotte 41
Charles V 10
Charles VIII 10
Clinton Avenue 84-5, 96
Cohen, Miriam 52, 59-61, 99
Cove Road 65
Cove School 74, 111
Covello, Leonard 21-24, 26-
  30, 32-34, 43-51, 64
Cubetta Stadium 84

DeConde, Alexander 11, 60, 99
Dore, Grazia 15, 99

Ellis Island 62, 71, 87
England 9, 19, 21
Ets, Marie Hall 87-8, 99
Ewen, Elizabeth 52-3, 89, 99

Fiore, Carmen Anthony 6
France 9-10

Gabaccia, Donna R. 32, 34-
  8, 42, 58-9, 99
Gambino, Richard 9, 11, 39-
  45, 47
Garibaldi, Giuseppe 12-3, 17

Handlin, Oscar 3-4, 94-5
Hapsburgs 10-1
Hartford 61

Iacuzio, Dominic 83-4
Iacuzio, Emiddio 125
Iacuzio, Medio 84
Iorizzo, Luciano J. 2, 100
Interlandi, Anna 65-6, 74,
  80, 90
Interlandi, Michael 74, 90
Italy 2, 4-6, 7-21, 24, 27, 30,
  34, 41, 47, 56-57, 60-4, 66-
  7, 71, 74, 91-2, 95

Kessner, Thomas 5, 95, 100
Kraut, Alan M. 2-3, 100

Lanzare, Candida vii, 60,
  62, 88, 90, 91, 104
Lanzare, Rosina 121
Lanzare, Sabatino 121
Lauteri, Vincenza 122
Leone, Antoinette vii, 66, 91
Leone, John 71-2
Lobozza, Carl 62, 100

Mangione, Jerre 9, 11, 14,
  17-8, 21, 30, 86-7, 100

Marseilles 83
Mazzini, Giuseppe 12
Mazziotti Gillan, Maria 97
Merola, Lorenzo 124
Mezzogiorno 13-4, 17, 38, 44, 53, 55
Morreale, Ben 11, 100

Naples 1, 9, 11, 13, 17, 20, 65, 70, 89, 94
New Haven 62, 100
New York 1, 61-2, 65, 70-1, 73, 83

Pacific Street 63, 75, 91
Paris 17
Perrot, Michele 69
Pope Pius X 69

Risorgimento 12, 23, 27, 99
Rolle, Andrew 1, 100
Ross, Fiorina 82, 92
Russo, Alphonse 76, 78-9, 93
Russo, Raphael 76-7

S.S. Giovanni 70-1, 100
Salerno 9, 29, 62, 66, 68, 82, 89
Seller, Maxine Schwartz 86-7, 90, 100
Sgritta, Alphonse 6, 62, 64-5, 95, 106
Sgritta, Carlo 53, 64-6, 88, 90, 95
Sgritta, Dominic 13, 20, 29, 53, 64-7, 70, 74, 78, 83-4, 94 103
Sgritta, Matteo 65, 70, 72

Sgritta, Rosina 62, 64, 80, 82, 106
Sgritta, Salvatore vii, 60, 62-6, 71-2, 74-5, 77, 80, 82-4, 88-9, 91-2, 94-5, 104, 110, 122, 130-2
Sgritta Cerulli, Vincenza Giovanna (Jennie) vii-iii, 7, 63-85, 90-6, 99
Sgritta Iacuzio, Candida (Candy) viii, 7, 72-8, 82-4, 88-91, 94, 99, 126-9
Sgritta Merola, Angelina 123-4
Sgirtta Sabatini, Anna 90
Suppa, Grace 63, 81-2, 92
Sicily 10-1, 13, 18, 51
Sorrentino, Angelina 20, 44, 64-6, 68, 70, 74-6, 85, 90-2, 107
Spain 9-10
St. John's Cemetery 64, 77
Stamford 62-5, 83-4, 89, 125, 139
Stillwater Avenue 78

Turin 14-5, 17

United States viii, 1-8, 18, 27, 39, 52, 60-2, 66, 71, 83, 88, 91, 94-5, 99

Vecoli, Rudolph 3-4, 95, 100
Victor Emmanuel II 12-3

Williams, Phyllis 54, 56, 100

Zia Katherine 67

About the Author

FRANCES CALKA-NORTON was born in Stamford, Connecticut in 1954, to John and Angelina (Cerulli) Calka. While close to her Polish extended family, her cultural heritage was defined by her lively, loud, and large Italian family. At her grandparents' house (John Cerulli and Jennie Sgritta), she sat with her cousins at the children's table on holidays, feasted on pizza fritta and pasta, and spent time there in the summer, sleeping in the big bed her mother had shared with her sister.

Frances was always an avid reader and student, so it was no surprise that she developed a love of history and family genealogy. She has spent over three decades studying the local history of Stamford, Connecticut, and the social history of Italian Americans. Her dream had always been to write a book about her Sgritta family.

She attended Sacred Heart University and graduated Summa Cum Laude with a Bachelor Arts Degree in History in 1997. The academic dissertation she wrote during that time under the direction of Dr. John Roney, became the basis of her book *Crossing Between Two Worlds*.

Frances also holds a Master of Teaching and Learning Degree from Nova Southeastern University, as well as the State of Connecticut administrators' credentials, which she earned in Sacred Heart University's Graduate Program. As an elementary educator in the City of Bridgeport Public schools, Frances spent several summers working as a member of the district's curriculum committee, developing meaningful educational experiences for third-

and fourth-grade students, focusing on local Bridgeport history and immigration.

Frances lives in Trumbull, Connecticut, with her husband Tom, her daughter Kate, and her very large fur babies, Ava and Glory. An avid genealogist, she continues ongoing research into the lives of the Sgrittas and Cerullis, as well her Polish and Irish family connections.

SPUNTINI

This book series is dedicated to the long essay. It includes those studies that are longer than the traditional journal-length essay and yet shorter than the traditional book-length manuscript. Intellectually, it is a light meal, a snack of sorts that holds you over for the full helping that comes with either lunch or dinner.

Anthony Julian Tamburri. The *Columbus Affair: Imperatives for an Italian/American Agenda.* Volume 1. ISBN 978-1-955995-00-9

Joseph Rocchietti. *Lorenzo and Oonalaska.* A Novel. Edited and with an Introduction by Leonardo Buonomo. Volume 2. ISBN 978-1-955995-01-6

Mario Vitti. *Una nuova e più grande Settefrati sul suolo d'America.* Edited by Anthony Julian Tamburri. Preface by Riccardo Frattaroli. Volume 3. ISBN 978-1-955995-03-0

CASA LAGO PRESS EDITORIAL GROUP

David Aliano
William Boelhower
Leonardo Buonomo
Ryan Calabretta-Sajder
Nancy Carnevale
Stephen C. Cerulli
Donna Chirico
Fred Gardaphé
Paolo Giordano
Nicolas Grosso
Donatella Izzo
John Kirby
Chiara Mazzucchelli
Emanuele Pettener
Mark Pietralunga
Joseph Sciorra
Ilaria Serra
Anthony Julian Tamburri
Sabrina Vellucci
Leslie Wilson

www.ingramcontent.com/pod-product-compliance
Ingram Content Group UK Ltd.
Pitfield, Milton Keynes, MK11 3LW, UK
UKHW032334131224
452011UK00005B/70